# WFH

# WFH

## SECURING THE FUTURE FOR YOUR ORGANIZATION

ANDREW MCNEILE
AND MARK HILLARY

WFH: Securing The Future For Your Organization

© Andrew McNeile and Mark Hillary 2021
All Rights Reserved
ISBN:  979 873 167 8957

Published by ThinScale Books
Dublin, Ireland

www.thinscale.com

ThinScale
The Media Cube
Kill Avenue
Dún Laoghaire, Co. Dublin
A96 X6X3
Ireland

www.thinscale.com

Author portraits all supplied by the authors.

Cover by: Giovanni Misagrande

ISBN:  979 873 167 8957

WFH: Securing The Future For Your Organization
© Andrew McNeile and Mark Hillary

The right of Andrew McNeile and Mark Hillary to be identified as the authors of this work has been asserted by them in accordance with the Copyright, Designs and Patents Act 1988.

All rights reserved. No part of this publication may be reproduced, stored in or introduced into a retrieval system, or transmitted, in any form, or by any means (electronic, mechanical, photocopying, recording, or otherwise) without the prior written permission of the publisher. Any person who does any unauthorized act in relation to this publication may be liable to criminal prosecution and civil claim for damages.

We dedicate this book to those who believed in WFH from the outset and worked to make it a reality before Covid-19 taught the world what is really possible……you all know who you are!

# CONTENTS

**About The Authors** .................................................... 9
**Foreword** ................................................................ 11
**Preface and Introduction** ........................................ 17

Chapter 1:   The BPOs Sent Everyone Home, But How Secure Is Your Data Now? ....................... 27

Chapter 2:   WFH Is Here To Stay, So How Secure Are Your Employees? .... 31

Chapter 3:   When The Auditors Arrive Will The CX Industry Deliver? .......... 37

Chapter 4:   Which Risks Are Elevated As Your Team Returns To The Office? ................................................. 41

Chapter 5:   Security Will Be The Key To Surviving In The New Normal .......... 45

Chapter 6:   Security In An Era Of Decentralization ............................ 51

Chapter 7:   What Are The Immediate Security Risks Of WFH? .............. 55

Chapter 8:   ThinKiosk And WFH Security - A Shout Out From Frost & Sullivan ............. 59

Chapter 9:   WFH And BYOD: Does It Make Sense To Send Laptops To Agents? ........................ 63

Chapter 10:  What Is The Road To CX Recovery And Normality In 2021? ..69

| | | |
|---|---|---|
| Chapter 11: | Work-From-Home Is Becoming A Long-Term CX Solution | 73 |
| Chapter 12: | The Hybrid Company Has Arrived And It's Fantastic News For All | 77 |
| Chapter 13: | You Don't Get WFH Security By Monitoring Workers On Their WebCam | 81 |
| Chapter 14: | WFH Is Going Mainstream, But Will Companies Also Explore BYOD? | 85 |
| Chapter 15: | WFH Is The New Normal - You Need A New Security Plan Now | 89 |
| Chapter 16: | Helping Relaxed WFH Workers To Be Secure | 95 |
| Chapter 17: | Help Your WFH Team To Keep Their Environment Secure | 99 |
| Chapter 18: | Conclusion And Closing Thoughts On WFH | 103 |

**References:** .......................................................... 113

**Appendix 1:** Along the Frictionless Plane: The Case of ThinScale ............................................................ 123

**Appendix 2:** Simplified Case Studies ...................... 133

# ABOUT THE AUTHORS

**Andrew McNeile,** is based in Dublin, Ireland. He is the Chief Customer Officer at ThinScale Technology. ThinScale is a Deloitte Fast50 (4th Ireland) and Fast500 (187th EMEA) winner.
Andrew graduated with a BA Hons from the University of Oxford.

http://bit.ly/amcneile
https://thinscale.com

**M**ark Hillary is a British technology writer and analyst, based in São Paulo, Brazil. He studied Software Engineering and has an MBA from the University of Liverpool.

Mark hosts the CX Files podcast - a weekly show focused on the future of customer experience. He frequently contributes to the global media, focused on technology and CX, with articles published by the BBC, Financial Times, Reuters, and Huffington Post.

Mark has written several books focused on technology. His first was titled 'Outsourcing to India: The Offshore Advantage' published in 2004 by Springer in Germany. He co-wrote 'Global Services: Moving To A Level Playing Field' with Dr Richard Sykes in 2007 for the British Computer Society.

Mark has advised several national governments on technology policies and has advised the United Nations on the use of technology for development in Bangladesh and Nigeria.

http://bit.ly/markhillary
http://carnabysp.com
Social: @markhillary

# FOREWORD

I started my company 25 years ago and right from the start, my team has always worked from home. Since then, I have worked with many companies across many different sectors, but one of the most interesting has always been the contact centers.

Some people might question this. Isn't a contact center just a big warehouse with people answering calls? It might look like this on the surface, but the reality is that this is the frontline of how any company builds a relationship with their customers. How you manage these interactions is the difference between success and failure.

Consumers today don't just contact companies to complain about a problem, they engage because they want to - they enjoy a relationship with their favorite companies. Think about those lines of people outside Apple stores every time they launch a new product - those people love the brand. It's not just a new phone or watch. It's integral to their lifestyle.

The Covid-19 pandemic created a sudden wave of change in the contact center industry. Although most governments ruled that these were essential workers - because many of the services they work on are vital - the companies still had to keep their employees safe. This meant that working from home became normal across the industry.

Companies that previously employed a few thousand work-from-home agents suddenly had to manage hundreds of thousands of people distributed across the world. All at home managing personal customer data on their laptops.

Some had no infrastructure in place and some had to scale up from a minimal solution to an enormous global system that allowed everyone to contribute and work from anywhere. This was an enormous test for the entire industry and it wasn't flawless, but in most cases the transition worked.

As I write, we can see the light at the end of the tunnel. Vaccines are being delivered and there is a sense that business life may return to normal in 2021.

But it will not be a return to 2019. No airline ever wants to make their customers wait 8 hours to speak to an agent ever again. The contact centers need to build greater resilience and security into their future operating model and this means that working from home is almost certainly going to be a permanent feature of the industry.

This means that network designers need to think much more carefully about how customer data can be safely shared across a network that will often involve many thousands of physical locations - including a kitchen table or spare room.

When I first heard about ThinScale I was taken aback. Here was an innovative set of tools that can help executives manage these security and network risks - and it comes out-of-the-box. Agents at home can use their own device safe in the knowledge that the ThinScale technology creates a completely walled-off safe space separating their personal system and their business applications and data.

The world has dramatically changed since 2020. When the British Financial Times newspaper polled company leaders[1] in February 2021 to ask about their plans to return to the office they could not find a single company planning a return to the traditional Monday to Friday work pattern. Every company said that a hybrid of work-from-home and the office as a hub would be their 'new normal.'

Not only does every company leader need tools such as those designed in Ireland by ThinScale, but they also need to think carefully about what else will change. Remote management means less supervision and requires more trust. Onboarding and training strategies need to go online. Hiring no longer needs to be restricted to those within commuting distance from the office - you can hire from anywhere. Employee expectations have also changed in the past year and many now expect far greater flexibility from their employer than they would have enjoyed before the pandemic.

The World Economic Forum (WEF) suggested five years ago[2] that emerging technologies would lead to a Fourth Industrial Revolution where tools such as Artificial Intelligence (AI) dramatically change how we work and live our lives. This is clearly becoming a reality today. Many companies have been forced to undertake a dramatic digital transformation just to survive the pandemic.

In 2016, the WEF chairman Klaus Schwab said: "The speed of current breakthroughs has no historical precedent. When compared with previous industrial revolutions, the Fourth is evolving at an exponential rather than a linear pace. Moreover, it is disrupting almost every industry in every country. And the breadth and depth of these changes herald the transformation of entire systems of production, management, and governance."

This prediction is now becoming our modern industrial reality. Every industry I can think of is being redefined by emerging technologies, from automobiles to airlines to publishing. But all these companies still need to communicate with their customers. The contact center will remain relevant even as automation, chatbots, AI, and working from home change how they look and function.

Innovative companies like ThinScale are the enablers, making it possible to embrace this wave of innovation and to ensure our information always remains safe. As our lives become more data-centric and mobile we need to know how to navigate safely through this new environment.

This book documents some of the ideas that Andrew and Mark have discussed about the changing nature of work and what it means to keep data secure in a distributed environment. It's a great way to start the conversation in your own organization because they don't labor on network security protocols and jargon - they talk about what security really means for your business and customers. I hope you enjoy it.

Shelli Ryan, APR, Fellow PRSA<br>
CEO, Ad Hoc Communication Resources<br>
Las Vegas, Nevada, USA<br>
April 2021<br>
bit.ly/shelliryan<br>
adhoccr.com

**REFERENCES:**

1. https://www.ft.com/content/d2ad4ae3-6b40-4051-a6fe-6f8a75924e30
2. https://www.weforum.org/agenda/2016/01/the-fourth-industrial-revolution-what-it-means-and-how-to-respond/

# PREFACE AND INTRODUCTION

"Work isn't something our people come to the office for, it's something they do. Effectiveness can't be measured by the number of hours people spend in an office. Instead, giving people the freedom to choose where they work will boost effectiveness. Giving our people more flexibility will support a better work-life balance and also help tap into new talent pools while keeping our existing band members."

Spotify blog post, February 12, 2021

In March 2021, Singapore Airlines announced[1] that the personal data of almost 600,000 of their loyalty club members had been compromised. They blamed the airline technology specialist SITA for the breach, although as BP discovered after the Deepwater Horizon explosion in 2010, you can't evade the flak by blaming a subcontractor.

As we write this introduction, the Singapore Airlines data breach is just the most recent in a long history of data breaches that are enabled by hacking, weak security, or incompetence. In 2013, Adobe managed to lose the personal information of 153 million customers when hackers accessed their system.

The hotel giant Marriott International announced in 2018 that the personal information of over 500 million customers had been accessed by a Chinese intelligence group seeking information on US citizens. In 2016, Yahoo announced that the passwords of all 3 billion users had been compromised. What made the Yahoo announcement worse was that they had known about the breach for several years. Verizon was in the process of acquiring Yahoo when they announced the breach and it immediately knocked $350 million off the value of the company.

These data breaches have a material impact on the affected companies, as Yahoo found out. Not only do regulators issue fines, but the damage to the reputation of a company can be so severe that some may struggle to survive.

In most cases, it is the damage to reputation that is the most destructive aspect of a data breach. Being featured on the evening news because you are not taking care of your customer data is not where any CEO wants to be.

The brand reputation specialist, Interbrand, published research early in 2021 estimating that $223 billion in brand value is currently at risk because of the possibility of security breaches - and this is only measuring large global companies.[3] Typically, the damage this type of security breach can cause can be quantified as 53% of net income in 2020.

This brand value damage cannot be understated. Telefonica losing their technology systems to the WannaCry ransomware attack or the explosion on BP's Deepwater Horizon rig show how the public can attach a brand reputation to a disaster for many years.

Understandably some companies prefer to keep data breaches quiet figuring that they can fix the problem and not alert customers or their industry regulator. Uber tried this[4] in 2016 when hackers accessed 57 million user accounts. They even paid a $100,000 "ransom" to the hacker in exchange for silence about the data breach. It didn't work as they were eventually hit with a $148 million fine - worse than they could have settled for if they had come clean.

We are not arguing that you should not trust these companies any longer. It's likely that the companies that have suffered a very public data breach may well have invested more in ensuring it never happens again.

The European Union is generally seen as a world leader in the regulation of data and defining how companies can use customer's personal information. The General Data Protection Regulation (GDPR)[5] implemented in 2018 establishes some strong protections for consumers and guidelines for companies:

- Companies must be explicit about when they are collecting personal data and why they are asking for it
- Companies must only retain data on customers for as long as it is actually being used
- Companies must limit their data collection to only what is necessary to provide the service they offer
- Companies must provide adequate security to protect the data

- Any customer can "ask to be forgotten" by requesting that the company erases all data on that individual

GDPR is gradually improving the regulation of data globally as many other regions are now improving their own data regulation in the shadow of the European gold standard.

But it's still not enough. Hackers are still out there targeting companies all over the world, even those with European operations and therefore following the procedures defined within GDPR. Some hackers are state sponsored, deliberately stirring up trouble or just trying to access consumer information from a different region.

Some are criminal and demand payment in return for the safe return of systems and data. In 2017, the British National Health Service (NHS) was crippled by a ransomware attack called WannaCry.[6] Medical appointments were cancelled and doctors across the country could no longer access their locked computers - they were asked to pay $300 to unlock each device. In the aftermath, it was described how 'basic IT security' could have prevented this malware attack.

We live in a world today where personal data is more valuable than ever. Companies are collecting more data and are increasingly analyzing it to improve their understanding of what their customers want and to create a more personalized service.

Services like Amazon Go are redefining how retail works[7], but while most attention is paid to the fact that their stores have no checkouts, the real value is in the behavioral data Amazon is collecting.

If Amazon knows everything about your shopping habits and correlates this with other variables, such as the weather and a major events calendar, then it's easy for them to send a time-limited special offer voucher that will be highly relevant to your lifestyle. Customers that regularly buy beer before major football matches will be delighted to receive a 24-hour 10% off beer voucher one day before a major Champions League game.

It's clear that companies are collecting more personal data and it is also clear that there is a global ecosystem of people that are eager to access this data. Company executives must therefore be aware of their responsibilities to their customers and must keep that data safe.

Traditionally this would be achieved by creating a 'firewall' - essentially building a big wall around the organization to prevent access unless the person using the data is inside the organization.

This approach became dated as cloud computing became popular. With data and systems stored in the cloud, some communication and transfer of data is essential so data will naturally move around through different systems, often in different countries.

This historic focus on the network and firewall creates a mindset that is focused on network-centricity. This thinking leads to a view that if my central data is secure and the perimeter of my network is secure, then everything is fine - my entire company is secure.

Analysts and security advisers endlessly recommend several layers of security, even for networks with a strong firewall. For example, security when transferring information inside the network - if this is weak then one single breach of the firewall means that there is absolutely no internal protection.

Simple data theft, such as that possible using key loggers or credential theft, can give a hacker the keys to the theme park if your network-centric view means that you are relying almost exclusively on the firewall. Think about these end points where users are actually working - think about the attack surface from the edge and not the center.

But more recently a new challenge has emerged and this will largely be the focus of this book - working from home.

The Covid-19 pandemic meant that almost every office-based professional was forced to work from home (WFH). It was an emergency response to enforce social distancing on entire populations and we should not forget that in the early days of the virus it was believed that a vaccine might require many years of research and development. Before Covid the fastest vaccine ever created was for mumps, and that took four years.[8]

Security managers had to tear up their existing strategies and figure out how to protect their core office environment, their cloud, and also the home Wi-Fi network of every employee in the company.

Originally these companies all expected home-working to be a short-term reaction to the pandemic. The general plan would be to revert to Monday to Friday back in the office once it became safe to return. But a year of flexible home-working has redefined employee expectations of employers.

In her foreword, Shelli Ryan mentioned that the Financial Times published a story on February 28th, 2021 where they contacted dozens of major companies to ask when they will resume life in the office again.[9] Every company, from PwC to Lloyds Bank to Aon to Revolut, said that they are now embracing hybrid work - so the option to continue working from home has been normalized by the pandemic.

The Financial Times could not find a single company that said they are returning to a traditional five-days-a-week in the office. We believe that this will actually become a normalized employee expectation and any CEO attempting to return to the standards and practices of 2019 will find it a struggle to attract the best talent.

This WFH revolution dramatically affected the customer service operations in every industry. Contact centers are traditionally large buildings crammed full of agents in long rows of desks. It's no surprise that they could not operate in the middle of a pandemic.

All of the major global contact center companies sent their people home with a laptop and asked them to continue working from home. In some places like the Philippines, where home Wi-Fi networks are not as ubiquitous as they are in Europe or the US, the employers worked directly with telecoms companies to ensure all their employees could get online.

The Global Teleperformance Group is a good example. They had a few thousand agents working from home before the pandemic. Once it was clearly not safe to work in a contact center they managed to keep their operations running with around 250,000 agents connecting from home.

Obviously all office-based employees will be affected by the WFH trend, not just contact centers, but customer service operations are naturally an environment where data security is important. Customer interactions involve accessing personal data and often involve payment details. It's critical that all this is secure.

Designing a WFH security strategy that helps employees to always maintain secure standards, even without effort, is extremely important. TechRepublic magazine published a feature in June 2020 arguing that around half of all home-based workers are less likely to follow security protocols specifically because the boss is not watching them.[10] You can't design security systems that require everyone to remember how to stay secure - it has to just be there all the time, baked into the process of just doing your job.

It is also critical to respect the rights and privacy of the home worker. If a company has asked the home-based employee to provide their own IT equipment then the same security solution that ensures security when being used by the company should also ensure privacy for the employee - the company should not be able to snoop around on their employee's computer. In effect, there is a wall between the operating system the individual uses when using their equipment at home and the system used when working.

This book is a series of eighteen short essays. It's not focused on the detailed technology of security, but each essay explores a different question around this theme of how to rebuild companies so they can be secure when WFH has been normalized. The world of work has changed forever and new methods are required to ensure that data can remain secure in this new environment.

Whether your team is at the office or working from their bedroom, every executive needs to feel secure that the reputation of their company will not be destroyed by a data breach that was easily avoidable.

In the post-pandemic world, WFH is here to stay. It's time to embrace what this means for the way your company is structured.

We hope you enjoy the book. Please feel free to contact either of us via the LinkedIn profiles listed on our author pages.

Andrew McNeile
Mark Hillary
April 2021

## CHAPTER ONE:

# THE BPOS SENT EVERYONE HOME, BUT HOW SECURE IS YOUR DATA NOW?

Business Process Outsourcing (BPO) faces a crisis. The Covid-19 pandemic has made it impossible, or extremely difficult, to work in contact centers. Social distancing rules and stay-at-home orders have led to most BPO and customer service companies sending all their contact center agents home with a laptop. Working from home is the new normal.

Some of the bigger companies sent tens of thousands of their employees' home. They have all been talking about the heroes that made it happen and flooding LinkedIn with stories of success - we kept going, despite the virus, is the general message coming from all of them.

But the honeymoon is over.[1] The business media is full of stories explaining just how difficult managing a remote workforce really is. You cannot just setup a Virtual Private Network (VPN) and send everyone home with a laptop. These agents are usually handling customer data, often highly personal information. The companies managed to keep the agents answering calls, but they almost certainly compromised security standards.

Soon, your auditors will be visiting. Let's imagine what some major clients are going to say to their customer service providers:

- "Well, it seems you are delivering everything securely without the need for a contact center, so when are we going to receive some concessions? You no longer have all those capital costs so your customers should be rewarded."
- "What do you mean; you can no longer meet the security Service Level Agreements (SLAs) because your work from home environment doesn't have the right data security protocols?"
- "Why am I reading a story in the New York Times about my customer's personal data being offered for sale online?"

There will be some difficult boardroom conversations in the near future.

Some of the BPO companies are running their own security audits, or being forced to run audits by their clients. Will their work from home infrastructure pass the test or will they even publish any unfavorable results?

One of the biggest challenges is scalability. At the start of this year, nobody expected that entire companies would need to switch to a work from home model. When different national leaders started announcing quarantine measures these companies had to buy equipment and rapidly get everyone ready to work from home. Security standards were a long way down their to-do list when their ability to survive the crisis was being challenged. So now that they have everyone working from home, are the security protocols they rushed out overnight safe enough and can they be scaled as the team size changes?

Here's an idea. If you run a company that is working with a BPO to manage your customer service then why not send some of these questions to your account manager:

1. How can you guarantee that only your agents are logging in to your systems?
2. Are all communications encrypted, so if someone hacks the Wi-Fi an agent is using there is no way to monitor or collect personal customer data?
3. Are your agents trained in the signs that may indicate a potential cyber breach?
4. Have you audited the Wi-Fi security agents are using at home?
5. Are agents using personal apps, such as email, on the same device and potentially inviting a phishing attack?
6. Are agents culturally trained to think of security first? In the office environment it's usually assumed that an IT security team has it under control, so who is managing it across thousands of homes?

That's just a start, but these are the most obvious questions you need to ask. All the BPO companies moved thousands of people into a work from home environment almost overnight. They had no time to plan for the security of a diverse network and although their heroic efforts meant that they kept on delivering services, it also meant that there will almost certainly be data breaches. The business press is already warning their readers to expect the worst.[2] 93% of data breaches take less than a minute and are usually not discovered for weeks.[3]

How secure is your customer data? It's worth asking. Now.

## CHAPTER TWO:

# WFH IS HERE TO STAY, SO HOW SECURE ARE YOUR EMPLOYEES?

Work from home is going mainstream. It was deployed on an enormous scale during the Covid-19 pandemic so employees across the world could observe quarantine at home and still continue to work productively for their companies.

This phenomenon was not limited to customer service and contact centers. Companies from just about every industry you can name were affected - a global virus pandemic doesn't trouble those in retail, but then leave those in construction alone.

The CEO of Barclays Bank has now indicated[1] that 'big offices may be a thing of the past.' Mark's wife works at a company in São Paulo that used to have over 1,000 people in their super cool city center WeWork office - one of those with free beer in the lobby. Now they have been told that working from home is to be extended indefinitely. This is a message going out to millions of people globally - you can stay at home forever.

Naturally the 'new normal'[2] will involve some people returning to offices, but we don't believe there will be a sudden rush[3] and many of those now working at home will be permanent. In the customer experience space there are companies such as 5CA[4] and LiveXchange[5] now enjoying the spotlight because they were always work-from-home companies. Most will go hybrid now.

So the new normal will involve many more work from home employees across all industries, but this is particularly noticeable in customer service. Most contact centers are crammed full of people. Even as they are now opening again and scaling up, they cannot go back to full capacity because of social distancing guidelines.

All those companies will need to offer a blended solution of some people in the contact center, some working from home, and some digital transformation that can automate a percentage of the usual call volume - or improve self-service options so the customers never even need to get in touch because a Google search had all the answers.

This means that there will certainly be an issue with information security in the industry. Every customer service company rushed to get all their agents working from home overnight. In some cases that meant organizing for tens of thousands of people to have the equipment and connectivity and all within the first days and weeks of the crisis in 2020.

The emphasis was always going to be on speed and business continuity, but now that we are facing into the future again, security must be a serious consideration. There is an assumption that remote workers are secure, but what about the endpoints

- the connection to the network? In all this rush, mistakes must have been made. We talked recently to the principal analyst of TrendzOwl, Stephen Loynd[6], and he told us that the leading customer service companies, such as Sykes, Transcom, and Teleperformance, have been able to rapidly scale their Work-at-Home deployments while maintaining the highest security and compliance requirements (e.g. PCI compliance). However, this leaves a lot of uncertainty across the wider industry.

It's not just customer service employees that are at risk, but there is a particular focus on this sector because these employees handle personal customer data, including payments. Anyone that wants to hack into some valuable customer information - such as a list of payment card data - will start with the customer service function.

It's important to step back and review all your processes from the perspective of working at home. It appears that the possibility to work as normal will return during 2021, but many companies will deliberately choose to continue supporting home working so they can build greater resistance.

Every stage of the customer interaction needs to be reviewed with the audit specifically asking the question, how do we make this safer for home-based workers? For example, if a customer is using an existing payment card then there is no need for an agent to see the entire card details - the last 4 digits is enough. These principles are well established, but this level of systems thinking has to be applied to all processes - not just one area.

All authorization and approval processes need to be anonymized and have automated unpredictable routing to avoid any illicit collaboration between employees. This keeps the employees safe, but also ensures the customer data is entirely safe. Revamping and reviewing your business operations with a work-from-home lens is essential to maintain complete compliance and security.

The immediate crisis has passed - now it is time to ensure that business can be continued securely with remote workers, not just delivered during a crisis. It's essential to know about the home environment being used, the type of Wi-Fi security in place, and the login procedures that validate it is really the company employee accessing customer data.

But there is also one area we would emphasize that goes beyond all these logistical security processes - culture. You need to introduce a culture of security to all employees, especially those working outside the office. Many office-based workers are fairly oblivious to information security because "that's what the IT department manages." It's wrong inside the office and even more wrong when you have workers scattered all over the country.

If your team is not aware of how hackers generally attempt to gain access to systems and are not alert and reporting any suspicious activity then your expensive firewalls and other network security may be useless. Even Jeff Bezos was hacked[7] because he clicked on a link sent to his phone from someone he trusted. If you are using a private VPN, but the remote workers can still open a web browser when logged into the corporate system then your weakest link is exposed.

Building this culture of security needs training, it needs constant communication, and it needs the IT team to demonstrate that they are listening to all those reports from the team. Once they start ignoring potential security alerts coming from the remote team, the remote workers will stop bothering to report them.

    Work from home is here to stay. It most acutely affects the customer service industry, but every company with workers now handling company data at home need to consider this. How secure is your business environment and how might a phishing attack open your entire network to hackers?

## CHAPTER THREE:

# WHEN THE AUDITORS ARRIVE WILL THE CX INDUSTRY DELIVER?

Has your auditor checked on security protocols since the pandemic began or are you still using it as an excuse for weak security?

That's all changed. Q2 2020 was probably the most disruptive we have ever seen in our lifetime and when the statistics on closed businesses and unemployment dwarf the American Great Depression then you know this is going to be big.

Your next audit will be particularly important for every company delivering customer experience (CX) services. In this sector, almost every company had to rapidly move thousands of contact center agents from the office to their home.

Auditors for companies working in regulated industries will be particularly focused, during the next audit round, on any compliance failures caused by the new operating model. Every CX company will be doing the best they can to ensure that service levels remain the same, but the middle of 2020 saw such an enormous shock to the system that it will be no surprise if auditors zero in on the potential for information security weakness.

I expect the auditors are going to have a long list of questions, including:

- How much was spent on the immediate crisis, providing personal protective equipment for example?
- How will your ongoing costs change in future, if you need to keep on supplying masks, alcohol, and increasing office cleaning?
- Are the contact centers viable now that we still need to follow social distancing rules?
- If the configuration can be changed then how long will it take to get people working back in the contact centers again?
- Is the future going to be a blend of work from home and the contact center?
- If you are reducing your use of contact centers then are the prices going to be revised?
- How secure is my customer data in this new operating model?
- I know this had to be done to manage the crisis, but what is the road map out of this - what will the new normal really look like for my customer service team?

The CX industry performed incredibly well in 2020 and kept the show on the road. Many of those contact center agents were answering calls from worried airline passengers or citizens calling a government helpline. If CX went down then the impact on many hard-hit industries could have been even worse.

It's worth noting that the reality for many companies was not quite as their marketing teams presented it - all those heroes working long hours to ensure the company could keep going. Many companies were scrabbling for PCs, loading them into taxis for delivery to agents, and allowing agents to access sensitive systems from remote machines until the situation could be controlled..

But it's now time to explain, what happened, how information security has been prioritized, and where the 2021 road map begins. Endpoint security was often overlooked in the rush to keep companies going because the focus was on central security, but this is a dangerous way of thinking about security as it leaves the edge of your network exposed. No company can survive in crisis mode forever. If social distancing is going to be an accepted part of office life for the next few years then companies with large contact centers need to create a plan for how they will look in future.

Your next audit is only the beginning because many countries are still in lockdown (as of writing this in early 2021). Some are trying to emerge from their quarantine measures even though cases of the virus are rising - there is a clear message that business can only take this pause for so long. As companies restart, auditors will want to know how employees and customers are being protected and how operating models might change in the medium term.

Get ready for a barrage of questions because clients that were grateful for heroic efforts during the immediate crisis of the pandemic will now want to plan the future for their customer service operation.

## CHAPTER FOUR:

# WHICH RISKS ARE ELEVATED AS YOUR TEAM RETURNS TO THE OFFICE?

When the pandemic struck, the initial instinct of every business leader was survival. In contact centers globally the first step was to get everyone home, get some equipment out to them, and ensure they could continue to manage all the normal customer interactions on calls or chat from the home environment.

There are some amazing stories from across the industry of contact centers that spent millions on equipment to ensure they could keep going. They achieved that immediate goal and they survived. The next phase was to stabilize the environment. The information security teams started tightening security and ensuring that what had been an immediate response could be scaled into an ongoing - and safe - delivery model.

But many companies have started returning teams to the contact center. It makes sense because not everyone has the space or privacy to easily work from home, and not everyone even wants to work at home 100% of the time. Many clients are looking to keep some agents at home so they can build a more resilient customer service function in future, but that allows contact center executives to start building out a longer-term strategy where service delivery is blended between home-based agents and the contact center.

But what are the difficulties as offices and contact centers open up again? The obvious ones are related to hygiene and social distancing. People cannot be crowded extremely close to each other at their workstations and they may need controls on the flow through the office - one-way traffic systems and better controls over shared spaces like kitchens.

But what about the technical issues? Just think how many of those WFH laptops are about to be brought back into the office and connected up to your corporate network. How many of them are now going back and forth - a day in the office, then a few days at home?

The cybersecurity company Tessian recently published research[1] suggesting that 52% of employees asked to work at home by their employer are engaging in riskier behavior than they would find acceptable in the office environment. Examples such as sharing confidential files via email, rather than more secure and trusted systems, are common because employees feel under less scrutiny at home.

The Tessian research said: "In some cases, employees aren't purposefully ignoring security practices, but distractions while working from home – such as childcare, room-mates and not having a desk set-up like they would at the office – are having an impact on how people operate. Meanwhile, some employees say they're being forced to cut security corners because they're under pressure to get work done quickly."

The tech journal ZDNet published a list of five key areas[2] that technology administrators need to focus on as thousands of WFH agents all start to blend their time between the contact center and home:

1. **Mixing work and play:** Zoom for work or Zoom for the pub quiz. These devices may have been used with many apps not usually found in the corporate environment.

2. **Not applying security updates:** without the security team watching closely, many security patches may have been missed or ignored.

3. **Free-for-all with laptops:** it's important to confirm every person with access to the corporate laptop - sensitive details may have been left on a screen as a partner or child does some online shopping.

4. **Dirty devices:** physical cleaning of all devices and developing new habits about the use of smartphones and laptops - they carry a lot of germs.

5. **WFH habits at the office:** expectations of freedom with corporate equipment may transfer back to the office - the IT team will be deluged with requests to use unauthorized applications.

This is a useful checklist, but it will need to be augmented, especially if some employees are now going to be blending their time between the contact center and home - it creates a new type of network security requirement.

It's worth remembering that a lot has changed since 2019. You are probably going to be working with a blended environment now - there are few companies that are work at home only or office-only. Your business processes all need to be reviewed with this in mind and it's likely that some need to change to embrace the post-pandemic environment - to improve security, but also process flow.

If most WFH agents are ignoring security protocols then it's essential to explore a technical solution that can physically lock down devices when used away from the contact center, in addition to a communication strategy that reinforces why security is essential and how everyone can contribute to a secure work environment.

## CHAPTER FIVE:

## SECURITY WILL BE THE KEY TO SURVIVING IN THE NEW NORMAL

It's time to get back to business. Every corporate leader can understand why there was a need for a lockdown. At the time it looked like the best way to fight the spread of the new Covid-19 pandemic, but unfortunately the virus is still out there and although vaccines are going into arms, the long-term consequences remain unclear.

A failure to adapt cannot be an option if you want your business to remain operational. Even with a global vaccine rollout underway, 2020 has changed attitudes and approaches to work practices - especially the acceptance of working from home as normal and possible to support.

It's time to plan for the future, not just for a return to normal, but to embrace what has changed and to accept it.

The Choluteca bridge in Honduras gives a nice analogy. In 1998 Hurricane Mitch hit this 300-meter bridge across the Choluteca river. The bridge survived largely unscathed, but the roads at either end of the bridge were completely washed away - there was no trace that the roads had even existed. The hurricane was so powerful that it carved out a new path for the river so the bridge was left there with no connecting roads and no longer spanning a river. Locals started calling it the bridge to nowhere and it took over five years before it was reconnected to the highway.

That's the danger for companies and company executives that are resistant to the concept that there will be a post-pandemic new normal. Employee expectations around flexibility have been increased, nice-to-have work/life balance measures are now becoming normalized and expected. Many executives are also embracing the tremendous opportunity to hire from anywhere.

The Choluteca bridge became irrelevant. Could the same happen to your business?

There are many examples of the new normal out there. In the UK, local convenience stores are booming.[1] Many business leaders are complaining that the reduction in commuting is destroying city centers, but local stores and cafes in the suburbs are now getting all that business instead.

We heard a great example[2] of a small family-run tofu store in Singapore that pivoted to delivering fresh tofu - unheard of before the pandemic. Now they are selling more than ever. Even 5-star hotels like Claridge's in Mayfair are finding that people will spend a lot of money to have their food delivered to homes on the back of a motorbike. CFC, or Claridge's Fried Chicken[3] isn't a brand any of us expected to know in 2019.

Almost every company offering professional services has moved their employees into a home environment. There are now some governments and leaders[4] calling for people to get back to their "normal" working environment because businesses that rely on commuters going to city centers depend on them.

Really? We need to save the coffee bars?

This is short-sighted - the change has already taken place. Andrew recently spoke to a senior executive in a major technology company about another executive working within the customer service industry. The customer service executive had said that when this pandemic blows over he expects to see a maximum of 25% of his employees continuing to work from home,. The tech executive immediately said "wow, that company will be really uncompetitive then!"

That's the reality. Some executives still don't get it. They still can't see that their entire business ecosystem has changed, even their supplier network will have been transformed. If you don't review how your business functions in this new environment then you are going to become uncompetitive - the entire business landscape has been changed by this pandemic.

For employees, it's not just about the flexibility to start later because they are no longer commuting, home-working is also preferred by many because it is more meritocratic. The people who deliver are the ones who do well - not those who spend hours in the office looking like they are contributing. Working from home destroys presenteeism and ensure that the best contributors to the team are the ones that are noticed.

Destroying presenteeism and the office 'favorite' also comes with far greater flexibility. You need to finish early on Friday to travel somewhere. No problem, so long as all your expected work has already been delivered. No need to beg the boss to let you leave an hour earlier than usual and then be cat-called by colleagues calling out 'part-timer' as you leave the office.

For companies to effectively facilitate working from home, executives need to consider more more than just a laptop on the kitchen table. Greater transparency about how decisions are made. Improved communications. Mental health support for employees who prefer a more social workplace - the list can go on, but just like Maslow's hierarchy of needs emphasizes physiological needs as the most basic - food, water, shelter, etc - we believe that security is the most basic need for an effective work from home strategy.

You can design a new remote working model and improve communications, but without a redefined security model the entire edifice could come crashing down with all the repetitional risk that a loss of customer data can cause.

Companies rushed to move office-based workers to their home as the lockdown and stay-at-home orders swept across the world in 2020. Business continuity was more important than security. Now it's clear that many workers like this new flexible work environment and they want it to remain, so a complete security review should be top of the agenda.

Getting back to business and building a recovery into the 2020s is now the priority for all these companies with armies of workers based at home. Ensuring that security is adequate for this operating model to become permanent is now essential.

I haven't heard about any major security disasters in 2020 specifically caused by home working, but security firms such as McAfee[5] have detected very specific hacker activity. They are targeting companies with large numbers of home workers so it's only a matter of time.

Business continued through the lockdown. Now you need to ensure that it can continue for the long-term. We are entering a new normal and that means all your security procedures need a complete review.

## CHAPTER SIX:

# SECURITY IN AN ERA OF DECENTRALIZATION

Human-centered design will be at the heart of a new era of decentralized companies that allow workers to contribute from an office, a shared working space like IWG (formerly Regus) or WeWork, or from their home.

As Fast Company has documented[1], this requires new thought around public spaces, our work environment, and our homes. We need to think about how our working life has changed as well as the changes to many other aspects of consumer behavior - such as the dramatic growth in e-commerce during the pandemic.

Consider this research[2] by McKinsey. They are suggesting that consumer behavior has been dramatically impacted by these 5 trends[3]:

- Shift to value and essentials
- Flight to digital and omnichannel
- Shock to loyalty
- Health and 'caring' economy
- Homebody economy

The effect of these trends is staggering. 40% of American consumers now plan to spend less and to focus more on essentials, such as groceries and household supplies. American e-commerce saw the growth expected over the next decade in the quarter after the first lockdown. 60% of customers globally have switched brands and this is 75% in the US. This is because trusted brands did not pivot to offer more convenient or safer delivery options during the pandemic. More than 70% of the people McKinsey talked to are being far more careful when away from their home.

Taken together, these trends point towards a far more decentralized society and economy in future. We have seen retailers respond immediately, but this is also going to profoundly affect other sectors such as healthcare and education. Companies like McKinsey are suggesting that industries now have to adjust to a decentralized world or face a very uncertain future - or any future at all.

The contact centers and all other professional service companies that switched into a work-from-home model urgently need to review their security. But what about the schools and universities? What about the doctor's offices and hospitals?

This question of security runs far deeper than just the contact centers alone. There is a need for a completely new approach to information security that embraces a decentralized society. Consumers and workers are more likely to be working, shopping, and consuming remote services from their home yet millions have probably never even changed the password on their Wi-Fi router, let alone considered security in more detail.

McKinsey has estimated[4] that in the US alone we will see Telehealth explode from an industry worth about $3 billion a year to about $250 billion. That's just one part of the healthcare industry growing from a few billion to quarter of a trillion dollars. Who is considering the security implications of all this?

In the immediate future it needs to be you. The great challenge is on that last mile between the home worker and their nearest exchange. You need to be asking questions around which PC or other equipment is being used, what router is being used, what Internet speed is being used? The real value that ThinScale's validation tool offers here is the ability to eliminate many of these variables.

The need for greater security is required across all of society. We need to understand the importance for security because of decentralization and working from home in the same way that most people now understand phishing. OK, some people still click on those links, but the majority of people understand that there is a need to be vigilant when "your bank" emails or calls and asks you to respond with your PIN.

This needs to be an important component of your training program for home-based employees. Securing the network is not focused solely on the technology and network systems required for security, there is also a need to build an information-secure culture and that means teaching your people how to think constantly on security.

Information security also needs to enter a new normal. It's now the responsibility of every home-based worker and consumer. We need to enter a new age where security is understood by everyone.

## CHAPTER SEVEN:

# WHAT ARE THE IMMEDIATE SECURITY RISKS OF WFH?

Information security needs to enter a new normal. We cannot enter into a new environment where business decentralization is normal without entirely redefining how we keep information safe.

But the frontline at present is the work-from-home community. All those workers sent home during the pandemic and now based at home. There are many companies now announcing that working from home is permanent[1] and many waiting until later in 2021 to decide. What is very clear is that even those that adopt some form of hybrid solution are going to dramatically alter how their offices function[2] - because they will almost certainly accept that some people are never returning to the office.

A broad decentralization of society is taking place and this requires a new approach to information security, but the immediate risk is all these professionals sent home just to maintain business continuity. They are now based from home permanently, or at least long-term. What are the most immediate information security risks[3] to focus on?

- **Home Wi-Fi security:** using weak protocols, such as WEP, and even just never changing the admin password for the router means that anyone nearby can tap into a router and monitor network traffic.
- **Phishing:** the largest cause of security leaks and hacks. Even Jeff Bezos was scammed[4] when he clicked on a link in a WhatsApp message - he trusted the sender, but it goes to show that even the tech giants can be victims. It's important to have a clean system, perhaps an entirely separate personal and business system - no email or texts on the business system. Alternatively, using a secure 'tunnel' system so the computer in the home can access a remote system, but without any other software on the computer being able to penetrate the tunnel.
- **Passwords:** password security is obvious, but often ignored. It's critical that any application allowing access to corporate systems or customer information has a two-stage password procedure. This helps to guarantee that only the known employee can login, rather than anyone who copies the first password. Typically this might involve the employee registering their phone number with their employer and after the initial login they will need to do a second-stage login with a code that has been sent to their phone.

The real challenge here is that most home workers are not security experts. IT teams can send out advice on how to improve Wi-Fi security and how to spot phishing attempts, but they cannot control everything that goes on inside a person's home - for that it would in fact be easier to just get everyone back in the office.

What is needed is a way of making the device at home completely secure without relying on the home-based worker to do that. Just make it easy. This overview of the Secure Remote Worker product from Thinscale[5] by Michael DeSalles of Frost & Sullivan gives a good idea of the issues and a safer approach.

> "The rather small but dynamic ThinScale team disrupted the thin client market with **ThinKiosk** – the first Windows-based PC-to-thin-client converter – back in 2013. Quietly and effectively, ThinScale has empowered IT departments worldwide with software solutions that are mission-critical in today's modern digital workplace."

The remote worker can even use their own personal device because this approach uses centrally managed thin-clients. Basically, the remote device is only being used as a display for a system that is back in the office. Separating the different environments means that a remote worker can switch between their own device and the work environment, but there is no possibility of information being transferred between the two.

We believe it will be essential to take this approach as more and more workers are based from home. It's not enough to teach them about password hygiene and phishing attacks - people are human and they cannot be vigilant 24/7. If the system itself is protected then this creates a far better way to keep information secure.

These security reviews need to be taking place globally now because most of these home workers are not returning to the office anytime soon.

## CHAPTER EIGHT:

# THINKIOSK AND WFH SECURITY - A SHOUT OUT FROM FROST & SULLIVAN

The ThinScale CEO, Brendan Kiely featured on Mark's CX Files podcast in April 2020 - right at the height of the initial pandemic and lockdown.[1]

Brendan highlighted the initial response to the lockdown and although a lot has changed since that podcast episode, the emphasis on WFH has remained. WFH is now an ongoing business strategy for all of the contact centers and Business Process Outsourcing (BPO) companies.

In another CX Files episode from 2020, the industry analyst Michael DeSalles[2] of Frost & Sullivan explored the importance of WFH and how it will continue to be used into 2021. ThinScale has a lot of time for the advice of Frost & Sullivan and everyone in the company was proud to see F&S grant a major award to ThinScale just before the pandemic.[3] The 2020 Global Enabling Technology Leadership Award was awarded to ThinScale because Frost & Sullivan felt that this technology is essential for modern distributed workers - it's very timely right now.

Michael DeSalles was speaking about WFH on the CX Files interview and he started talking about ThinScale. Mark Hillary had just asked a question about remote workers using their own devices (BYOD) and how they can be used within a contact center environment - Mark's point was that it's surely unviable to keep shipping thousands of laptops to contact center agents at home.

Michael responded: "Check this out, I have a great story. In my research on this major shift, I found this small software company called ThinScale, and they're based in Ireland. And what I discovered is that ThinScale, for a long time has been a leader in architecting, and delivering software solutions that help organizations to effectively implement and manage their remote working right and BYOD and business continuity strategies."

This was a great shout out and the ThinScale team is grateful to Michael, although we are sure that the solution was front of mind for him because of the Frost & Sullivan award. He went on to talk about the ThinKiosk[4] solution and how it's a critical tool for contact centers that want to manage agent fraud when agents are working remotely because it allows the agent to only switch between their home mode or work mode on their device - nothing can be mixed.

It clear to us that WFH is not just an emergency response to Covid-19 - it is quickly becoming an important and standard component of the BPO delivery model. The BPOs will continue using contact centers, but the previous scale will never return. The future is a blended model that offers their clients much greater resilience against disruption like this pandemic.

    If you want to ensure that you can operate a blended WFH model and guarantee the safety of your customer data then you don't need to listen to anyone from ThinScale telling you how great the ThinKiosk solution is… listen to the Frost & Sullivan opinion on the CX Files podcast!

## CHAPTER NINE:

# WFH AND BYOD: DOES IT MAKE SENSE TO SEND LAPTOPS TO AGENTS?

In a 2020 episode of the CX Files podcast, Mark Hillary[1] talked to Michael DeSalles of Frost & Sullivan about the Business Process Outsourcing (BPO) roadmap into 2021. One of the things Michael said on the podcast was that the contact center companies that had sent their employees home with a laptop during the pandemic were going to struggle to manage the amount of equipment they needed to order and maintain and how it would be smarter to pivot now to a smart Bring-Your-Own-Device (BYOD) policy.

Michael mentioned ThinScale in the podcast because they had recently won an innovation award from Frost & Sullivan for this exact type of service - securing BYOD laptops so they can be safely used by work-from-home (WFH) remote agents.

The contact center companies all had to send their agents home - there was no choice back in March 2020 - as this virus started taking over the world. They had to absorb the cost of thousands of laptops, and often broadband connections too. The question is, as we start accepting that WFH is now going to be a permanent component of a customer service strategy, do the BPO companies need to embrace BYOD?

Let's think about this logically. Some decisions were made in the middle of a crisis, but now we can see relative stability, what does it really cost to manage a contact center where all of your agents are working at home and you are providing the kit?

- Assuming 5-6,000 agents you would typically need to buy about 9,500 laptops per year (with an attrition rate of around 50 to 60% - plus delays, loss, breakages etc.)
- Shipping laptops around $18 each way
- Talking to BPOs, we estimate that around 10-15% of devices are permanently lost as agents move job, but only 60-65% are returned promptly - it's a real struggle to get them back
- All these delays means that about 20-30% more laptops are needed to cover for all the ones lost to agents or 'in the post'
- Requires a full-time laptop shipping team. For this size operation we would estimate about 1 manager, 3 regular employees and one temp - maybe 4 temps in busy periods. 2 employees full-time just managing retrievals.
- Average device reuse is about 5 agents, but maximum possible is about 10
- Cost benefit issues and damage to reputation if punitive measures are used to retrieve laptops. In short, it's not enough of

a loss to start sending in Rocky[2] so laptops are just written off

OK, now that sounds concerning, but let's look at some of the numbers. Remember, we are making quite a few assumptions here, but at the same time we think most of them are conservative - we are not trying to exaggerate this for effect.

- 9,500 laptops @ $600 = $5,700,000

Let's park that as an up-front cost, but think now about the operating costs.

- 10% of machines lost or damaged = $570,000
- Shipping 9,500 machines @ $36 each = $342,000
- Staff costs - approximately $300,000
- Additional machines to cover those in the post 1,500 @ $600 = $900,000

This is back of the envelope stuff, but it's easy to see that we are looking at ongoing operating costs of over $2 million. That's also ignoring the initial capex for the equipment and the cost of replacing damaged equipment. In short, it's a lot.

These costs will vary from country to country. We have heard that in some locations in Eastern Europe and Asia agents need to sign an employment contract that allows the BPO to withhold the cost of the laptop from their final salary payment if they don't return it. This will certainly not be legal in several other European jurisdictions though.

We have estimated many of these numbers, but believe they are a fair representation. It is worth pointing out a few additional variables that could influence this cost dramatically:

- We assumed 50-60% attrition and we all know contact centers where the reality is double this
- We assumed a center with about 5,000 people. That's a good size, but there are many companies with a bigger estate that this.
- Some BPOs are insisting that agents collect laptops from their local contact center. This removes the courier cost (although it's likely that agents will receive some compensation for collecting in person), but it also prevents the company hiring anyone that is not within commuting distance of the contact center - even if they are all working remotely. This ability to hire far and wide is a key benefit of WFH.
- Seasonality can play havoc with the number of agents required. If you need to scale up and down through the year to cope with surges then a lot of laptops will be just sitting in the cupboard.

We disappeared down this rabbit hole because Michael mentioned the ongoing value of BYOD. It seems to us that even if the contact center offers a grant or subsidy to help agents get their own equipment and then they need a software license to protect the BYOD device, it has to be more competitive that managing the logistics of handling thousands of laptops.

We know that contact centers had to manage their IT estate in the past, but WFH now presents many new options. Customer service companies have enough on their plate managing CX strategy. We don't think they need to also be building a logistics division - do you?

## CHAPTER TEN:

# WHAT IS THE ROAD TO CX RECOVERY AND NORMALITY IN 2021?

Work-from-home (WFH) is moving from the emergency response of 2020 to becoming a long-term component of any resilient CX strategy in 2021. But it is one thing to accept the truth in this statement and another to plan for a road ahead in which customer service and contact center companies look and behave considerably different to how they functioned in 2019.

When WFH was just an emergency solution, it required little more than a supply of laptops, a basic strategy to ensure the security of all these distributed workers, and reliable internet at the home of the agents. In some countries this was fairly simple, in some there has been a monumental effort by the Business Process Outsourcing (BPO) companies to work with telcos, so new installations are rolled out quickly.

We think that once it is accepted that a key part of the new normal in 2021 is going to be WFH as a long-term solution, there are several areas of planning and change that need to be addressed:

- **Security:** some of the larger BPOs had a good security strategy in place because they were already exploring WFH, but some just had to go with the flow of 2020 - it's almost certain that security was less important than business continuity, as Mark outlined in this recent article.[1] However, if this is now permanent, then a stable security strategy is required - customer data has to be secure in all working environments, including the home.
- **Management style:** remote management needs greater transparency about targets and metrics. Managers need to focus more on who is delivering and how. There can no longer be any consideration for who is making more of an effort by putting in the hours - this doesn't work in a distributed workplace. Tools like the Employee Net Promoter Score (eNPS) may be useful for tracking employee sentiment and this is about more than just employee wellbeing - happier employees are far more likely to create a secure remote work environment. If they are happy and engaged at work then they are far more likely to look out for the company and are less likely to ever consider becoming a bad actor and therefore opening up the risk of fraud.
- **Communication:** inclusivity is the key and managers need to take measures to avoid a hierarchy developing where some

workers are at the office and interacting with managers and some are 100% based at home. All decisions need to be taken and discussed openly in meetings. Meetings need to be recorded and available for those who missed one. An entirely new approach to online onboarding and training has to be created so new employees can be included without ever once visiting the office.

- **Culture:** a remotely distributed team needs to feel that their managers are open and transparent and decisions are defended and justified. This should always be true anyway, but it is even more important in a distributed environment because workers may feel isolated and detached from decisions if they are not included and explanations are not offered. Over-communication is preferable to not telling the team what is going on - and why.
- **Flexibility:** the commute to a contact center meant that split or short shifts were never easy to arrange, but if agents are at home then more flexible working arrangements can be explored. This might include GigCX or agents working across multiple accounts. The point is that there is a new possibility to build a more flexible customer service environment without the traditional contact center.

Much of the recent coverage of WFH has talked about the issues of agent isolation and how to manage remote workers effectively. There has been a lot of discussion around how to socialize remotely, with events like Zoom Happy Hours. We believe that a lot of these discussions miss the point entirely. This is no longer an emergency response. WFH is fast becoming an accepted and vital component of a customer service strategy.

The entire culture of organizations needs to embrace a distributed workforce - managers cannot behave as they did before the pandemic. They also need to move on from the emergency measures, such as handing out laptops to the agents. This is turning customer service companies into logistics specialists. Is that really where they should be focused?[2]

Building security into a distributed workforce has to be one of the most critical steps as CX companies accept that WFH is now permanent. Building a new culture that embraces transparency and values what each team member really contributes has to also be taken seriously. Getting the best from a distributed workforce requires a very different approach to traditional contact center management. The sooner the CX specialists recognize this, the faster they can transition into a genuine new normal.

## CHAPTER ELEVEN:

# WORK-FROM-HOME IS BECOMING A LONG-TERM CX SOLUTION

There has been a distinctive shift in the discussions around the use of a work-from-home (WFH) strategy in contact centers and Business Process Outsourcing (BPO). As the Covid-19 pandemic took hold in March 2020, the contact centers had to send their agents home, but the expectation then was always that this emergency response would eventually be reversed.

That is now being challenged. There is more and more promising news about the vaccine rollout each day, so there are hopes for some normality during 2021, but many corporate leaders have been thinking about their WFH experience. There are a number of reasons why the short-term WFH experiment may in fact become a long-term fundamental shift in the way that contact centers operate.

Here are just a few reasons why:

1. **Changing Expectations:** we know that some people find it hard to work from home because they don't have enough space or privacy, but the past few months have shown that the majority of people really value the flexibility. Nobody is missing their commute to the office so a more flexible approach to office hours is likely to be an employee expectation when looking for a new employer now. Don't expect to hire the best if you are insisting on nine-to-five in a downtown office Monday to Friday.

7. **Changing profiles:** new hires into contact centers that are already focused on WFH when they start are starting to reflect a different profile - they are slightly older and much more likely to own or rent their own home. This has interesting implications for contact centers because it means that agents have more insight and life experience. Smart companies will tap into these profile changes.

8. **Wider pool of expertise:** a huge benefit with WFH that remained fairly under the radar before the pandemic is that you can literally hire from anywhere - so you can raise the bar on who you do hire. You are not restricted to the people within commuting distance of your contact center. This can also have a positive effect on inclusivity because a large number of people who, for

various reasons, can't commute to a full-time job can now be considered.

9. **Multilingual and distributed:** the use of multilingual hubs is now being questioned by analysts. Why setup an office and hire people from all across a continent like Europe, bringing them all to one location? Why not just hire those people in their local markets to support local customers? Think about apps that are available globally on the app store and yet need to be supported in dozens of languages - you can easily tap into those skills in the regions where the customers need support.

10. **Security:** the greatest inhibition surrounding WFH before this pandemic was the fear that it's impossible to be secure when workers are distributed and based at home. This was clearly proven to be false and this acceptance opens up the possibility that this does not have to just be an emergency response. If it works better and it is secure then why not stay like this? The CX Files podcast episode with Andrew[1] focused entirely on this subject and especially how to move on from emergency mode into an acceptance of WFH.

11. **Resilience:** moving into 2022 we will see every Business Continuity Plan totally rewritten with the assumption that Covid-22 might be on the horizon. What if another unexpected pandemic sweeps the world? How would your company manage? Clearly the ability to WFH offers a dramatic

increase in resilience - whether it's blended with the use of offices or is now a 100% WFH strategy.

We think that we are going to see a very different customer service and contact center industry in 2021. There is a growing acceptance that even if some normality is restored, nobody will ever forget 2020. Every company leader will want to ensure that they will be resilient enough to withstand any future shocks and that is going to include the widespread continued use of WFH. This is now a part of the long-term solution for customer service globally.

## CHAPTER TWELVE:

# THE HYBRID COMPANY HAS ARRIVED AND IT'S FANTASTIC NEWS FOR ALL

The Davos World Economic Forum (WEF) 2021 focused on the future of work[1] and this is an appropriate time to explore how work is evolving because the Covid-19 pandemic has changed many long established traditions and expectations. The WEF analysis concludes that we may be entering a golden age for workers.

The three main conclusions of the analysis were:

- **Home working** is emerging as the preferred set up for many workers around the world.
- With a flexible definition of the workplace, it will be shaped around **worker preferences**.
- Prioritizing human **wellbeing** will be key for employers.

The pandemic forced many employers to ask their employees to work from home. Measures such as social-distancing and the reduced use of public transport all led to empty offices and workers getting used to a commute that involved little more than heading to the kitchen table.

The experience has largely been positive. Some employees have struggled with privacy and workspace and some have suffered isolation without the social activity of an office environment, but across the board most companies that worked this way found it was a success.

Now most employees want an assurance that their company will retain flexible working arrangements as the pandemic subsides. It's a win for the employees because even if they need to return occasionally to the office, they will now have far more control over where and when they work. Employers have found that this makes workers more productive and loyal - it's becoming a genuine win-win situation.

Flexibility also allows companies to build resilience into their operating model, to insure against any future disruption. A future pandemic, or even a more localized problem such as a flood or earthquake, will be far less damaging if the employees can easily work completely distributed from their homes.

The WEF advises corporate leaders to think beyond just the work from home element. There is an opportunity to build truly hybrid companies that have a much more positive culture than the working environment of 2019. The WEF analysis suggests five key opportunities that leaders can think about immediately:

1. Prioritize human health and wellness and evolve their mobility program to enable work from anywhere

2. Reimagine the future of the work post-COVID-19 and start building scenarios toward 2025
3. Explore "hybrid" workplace mobility for greater future resiliency
4. Consider global real estate portfolio transformation strategies with a liquid footprint to meet a dispersed workforce
5. Accelerate workplace technology transformation investments to enable a digital workforce

It is clear that the future will be hybrid. Executives that demand a return to the working practices of 2019 could face several problems, including negative publicity, the need to overpay to attract talent, and losing key team members who depart for a more flexible employer. The CEO of Goldman Sachs called working from home an "aberration" in February 2021 and the media attention swiftly turned on the long-hours culture in his company.[2] Security procedures need to move on from a pandemic footing to a normalization of a distributed workforce, but more importantly this is an opportunity to reshape our ideas of what it means to have a job and how to contribute to the mission of a company.

Corporate leaders have echoed platitudes such as 'our mission is our people' and 'we embrace work/life balance' for decades. Now is their chance to sweep away the slogans and to actually do it. The hybrid company has arrived and it is great news for both employers and employees.

## CHAPTER THIRTEEN:

# YOU DON'T GET WFH SECURITY BY MONITORING WORKERS ON THEIR WEBCAM

Is it really so much more insecure to allow your employees to work from home, compared to being in the office? Some analysts believe so. Research in the US[1] suggests that around half of employees working from home are less likely to follow safe data practices than if they were inside an office.

The report suggests that most managers trust their team, with 91% of IT leaders saying they trust that best security practices are being followed remotely. However, 52% of the employees said that they can get away with riskier behavior when working from home. In fact, 48% actually said that they don't follow best practices because the IT department is not watching. 47% say they just get distracted when working from home. 51% believe that data safety policies affect productivity and 54% look for workarounds in security policies make their life difficult.

We believe there are two key issues here:

- How do you create a working environment that is inherently secure without requiring endless password checks and other authentication that the worker will try to bypass?
- How do you create an environment where mistakes and distraction do not lead to a data disaster?

As the research suggests, people look for workarounds because they want to make their job easier. Half of the people in this study believe that security policies are preventing them from getting their job done.

Some managers are resorting to spying[2] on their employees. They ask for employees to keep their webcam and microphone on all day so managers can spontaneously ask questions - just like speaking over the top of a cubicle. Some install software that snaps photos from the webcam at random times, so the manager can see if the employee is consistently at their desk and working.

This isn't the answer though. In fact, it is likely to create a fear of surveillance that will lead to a decrease in productivity and attrition. After all, what kind of manager cannot adjust to judging their team members on deliverables and results, rather than expecting to physically check on progress every half an hour?

In any case, this idea that you can replicate managing-by-walking-about using cams doesn't even address the security question. How do you prevent distracted workers making expensive mistakes and create an environment where they cannot bypass the security?

The answer is to ensure that remote workers don't use local devices - it's impossible to police security on every remote device. The remote worker needs to use a device that has all local functionality locked down, so they access a corporate environment over a secure network. This ensures that they are doing nothing with any data remotely in their home; their device is simply accessing the corporate system and is unable to function locally when connected to the corporate system. A complete review of all processes used inside your organization, especially for functions such as customer service should identify these issues.

This is the type of Bring-Your-Own-Device (BYOD) strategy that smart companies should have been deploying back at the start of the pandemic. Some security websites are still talking about[3] Wi-Fi security and passwords, but the real issue is that the remote worker has to use a secure "tunnel" to the corporate system so all actions they take are on that system, not a laptop at home.

This avoids the problem of workers bypassing security procedures, making mistakes at home, and also helps to eliminate the potential for deliberate data theft - such as plugging in a USB key and downloading a client list.

If managers think that work from home security comes from taking photos on webcams then I'm sure their competitors will be delighted to read the news when a data breach inevitably occurs.

## CHAPTER FOURTEEN:

# WFH IS GOING MAINSTREAM, BUT WILL COMPANIES ALSO EXPLORE BYOD?

Mark wrote an article in 2020 about working from home and how the contact center suppliers and Business Process Outsourcing (BPO) companies might manage the need for new technology equipment in the home.[1] The main point was that it cannot possibly be economic to keep on supplying thousands of laptops - surely these companies will need to explore a bring-your-own-device (BYOD) business model eventually.

When Mark wrote that, we were still in the midst of the Covid pandemic and there was no sign of a vaccine. Since the various vaccine approvals started in December 2020 the situation has changed because there is now some light at the end of the tunnel. Although it may take most of 2021 to get the world vaccinated, at least we are not staring into the abyss of an incurable virus any longer.

But we have not seen any appetite from employers or employees to return to the standard operating model of 2019 - commuting five days a week to an office.

Take a look at the enormous insurance company Aviva.[2] They employ over 16,000 people in the UK. Their approach may be typical of many companies that employ professionals who can easily perform the same tasks at home. The company had two offices in York, now one is closing. The three offices in Norwich will become one soon, focusing their office presence in the city center.

Aviva is acknowledging that their team worked at home successfully during the pandemic so they will now enable a much more flexible working environment where employees can work at home or from an office - therefore the total office estate can be dramatically reduced.

New research in the US[3] suggests that only 11% of companies are planning to return to employees working full-time in an office. A survey by consulting firm PwC came to a similar conclusion, stating: "Executives and employees [are] converging around a post-pandemic future with a lot more flexibility, yet few are prepared to completely abandon the office space. The majority of companies are developing hybrid offerings in which people work from home some days and in their offices on other days." The same story is repeated in India[4], where employees of Deloitte now need to book a desk using a company app if they intend to visit the office.

The conclusion we are reaching here is that professional employees that perform their work on a laptop, contrasted with employees that need to perform a specific task like stacking shelves or dog-walking, are permanently going to expect working from home as a standard part of their contact.

Imagine being the boss that insists on your team attending the office every day when 9 out of 10 companies are offering flexibility.

This issue is developing far beyond the contact centers we have talked about earlier in this book. Deloitte[5] has 330,000 employees. PwC[6] has 276,000 employees. Accenture[7] has just over half a million employees. In chapter nine, we calculated the cost of supporting around 5,000 laptops as over $2m a year. It was not exact and there are plenty of variables, but the bottom line is that it is a lot.

We picked on these three companies just to illustrate the issue. They all employ intelligent professionals who will be doing their audit or consulting work on a laptop from their own office, a client's office, or their home. After the pandemic we expect that every company with this type of profile will be offering employees the ability to work from home.

The issue is not just the process of working from home, but the cost that surrounds this. What is the economic cost to your business of a running a device shipment service? What is the cost to the environment of procuring, shipping, recovering, reimaging, reshipping, and so on, over a 3 to 5 year cycle? Then you still need to dispose of the device. How can any company that builds a strategy like this also make claims about their contribution to fighting the climate crisis?

In many cases, companies are just using web access to their services so we really get the worst of all worlds. An expensive shipped device (to ensure security) with no actual level of improved security achieved.

So this issue about managing laptops is about to explode. Which major company will start exploring BYOD at scale? Their only alternative is to pass on these costs to their customers and we are sure their rivals will be happy to start undercutting their rates.

Many companies coped throughout 2020, but that was all. They continued to function, but were extremely vulnerable to security threats. The appetite for tolerating this threat has dramatically declined so you now need to find a dependable strategy that will allow BYOD to safely continue into the 2020s.

## CHAPTER FIFTEEN:

# WFH IS THE NEW NORMAL - YOU NEED A NEW SECURITY PLAN NOW

As Covid-19 spread from Asia to every other region of the world last year there was a wave of companies that all sent their employees home. We can remember many executives at the time talking of a two or three-week stint at home that would then be followed by a return to normal.

That never happened, but a lot more has changed and it's not always obvious without close examination. We don't think that we are now looking at a gradual return to how employees worked in 2019. The idea of this being a temporary bump followed by a return to normal has vanished because it has now been so long - people are getting used to the way things function now.

Work from home in the future will not look like it is today. We are still using a degraded version of what could be possible. People are suffering anxiety and loneliness as they struggle to work remotely without any options for travel or socializing. We should remember that work from home can be organized and used in a far more effective way than the Covid emergency response.

There has been a number of changes in the way that companies need to be organized and how people are managed. We cannot state strongly enough that this is a deep cultural change for many companies - this is far more than just moving from a centralized team in an office to a group of distributed workers mostly based at home.

Managers now need to focus on much more than just productivity. In recent research[1], 77% of executives said they would prioritize the wellbeing of their team over short-term profitability. Around half of all managers are now facing a challenge with employee wellbeing and mental health - issues that were certainly not their primary focus when the team was all in one place.

Managers caring for their team and not just ordering them to work harder is a very positive change, but it is one that requires certain skills from the managers - many companies will need to quickly focus on training and coaching so these changes can happen smoothly. Some managers may not like this new role.

This is why we believe that leaders will need to focus on the culture of their organization more than ever before. Claims about a "positive corporate culture" used to be something you would read in the annual statement. It read well, but the reality rarely matched up to the boardroom aspiration. With highly distributed organizations this does become a much more important issue, to prevent a two-track company[2] where those spending more time at the office may feel they are more important than home-workers, and also just to create a single sense of purpose.

Managing the culture of your organization will be more essential and more strategic when more employees are distributed from the central headquarters. Engaged employees are important for any business, but in the customer experience space, where we both spend a lot of time, it is critical - you can't have agents speaking to customers and giving the impression that they don't want to be there.

This has other implications too. Many companies hiring a customer service specialist now look very closely at the culture of their supplier for this reason. Who would hire a company to manage contact centers when you are aware that the agents who will be on the frontline are not well treated and paid rock bottom? Evidence of culture being embedded into the fabric of an organization is becoming an extremely important part of the B2B sales process.

This year has fundamentally changed how companies will be structured and managed. We can think of several ways in which this will have an immediate impact:

- **Employee expectations:** people are now going to expect flexibility in the workplace. WFH will be normalized. Companies will need to offer WFH flexibility if they want to attract the best people.
- **Office sizes:** why keep paying the rent on an office with 1,000 desks because you employ 1,000 people? Why not figure out how many are usually in the office day-to-day when they can choose to spend time in both home and the office. You might

- save 75% of your office costs. Lease terms mean that it will take time to realize the ideal real estate footprint, but check those terms and plan ahead.
- **Hiring globally:** it will be more and more common to hire highly skilled people who never have any intention of visiting the office. They will be hired for their skills, not their ability to commute. This raises the bar on who you can hire if you are searching for skills globally.
- **Focus on delivery:** managing a distributed team means that managers need to focus much more on deliveries - is the team delivering what is expected on time? There is far less focus on hours spent at the desk or how smart a team member looks in the office. This is a very democratic change and creates far more transparency inside teams. There is less scope for favoritism when team members are judged and measured based on actual outcomes.
- **We cannot turn back:** for all these reasons, and especially because employees now expect the pandemic flexibility to remain, very few companies will ever be able to return to their 2019 operating model.

The managers who still talk about a return to work structured as it was before the pandemic are living in a fantasy world. The world of work has changed beyond all recognition and WFH will now be an integral part of any corporate operating model. This means that your security procedures almost certainly need to be revised and remodeled.

This is no longer about an emergency response to the pandemic - this is now normal. We will see additional freedoms emerge over time, such as international travel becoming normal again and the ability to freely socialize. It's important to examine what has fundamentally changed and what is just temporary - such as travel restrictions.

WFH has become about much more than just working from home. WFH is now changing how managers manage and how culture is defined within enormous organizations. It was impossible to predict in 2019 that work/life balance and the flexibility to work from home whenever you want would be so important in 2021.

Like a tsunami, the pandemic has caused death, chaos, and destruction, but as the tidal wave has receded, and we mourn the loss, in the spaces that are created new life also emerges. One of these new shoots is an increased flexibility for employees all over the globe, something that so many people have wanted for so long is emerging as a common reality

## CHAPTER SIXTEEN:

# HELPING RELAXED WFH WORKERS TO BE SECURE

Salesforce is the latest giant company that has announced[1] that the work-from-home (WFH) emergency response to the Covid-19 pandemic is now becoming permanent. Salesforce employees will no longer need to rush into the office each morning because the management team are now allowing them the flexibility to choose where they want to work.

Salesforce is following a long list of companies that are realizing employees are going to be extremely unhappy if the new normal looks just like 2019. Employees have developed new working patterns and nobody likes to waste time commuting when it's unnecessary. The company can reduce the enormous amount of space they rent in San Francisco's Salesforce Tower[2] - although will they lose naming rights to the tower if they only have a few desks?

Workers love the flexibility that a WFH option provides, but how can you guarantee that a distributed workforce is completely secure?

You need to protect people from their own actions, because not everyone can be vigilant 24/7. Ten-pin bowling provides an easy analogy. When you go bowling with a friend who has never bowled before, or with a child, it's possible to add bumpers that shield the gutter on either side of the alley. This means that you can play without the fear of wasting balls by bowling them straight into the gutter.

Many researchers believe that people are naturally less secure when working from home. There are many reasons for this, but in general people are more comfortable at home, compared to an office - and also the boss is not watching. The threat of constant supervision, when you are sitting in an office, forces people to generally be more vigilant, but when at home you can be more relaxed about wearing pajamas to work and having a beer at your desk on Friday afternoon.

Around half of people[3] are so relaxed that they don't bother following the standard security practices that would be normal in the office. If you are relying on everyone to do the right thing then your network would not remain secure for very long - thanks to human nature.

So what you need is to create the 'bowling bumpers' for network security. You have to assume that no matter how many security guidelines you publish, people will not always follow them.

The most effective way to do this is to ensure that no data storage or processing activity takes place in the home. The home worker uses a device that is locked down so they cannot access the underlying operating system. The only way into the organization is through a secure tunnel into the apps and desktop tools within the corporate VPN environment. Secure Remote Worker by ThinScale[4] is an excellent example and has been highly praised by analysts[5], such as Frost & Sullivan, but even more importantly has been adopted by the majority of the worlds largest CX BPOs as their tool of choice to ensure BYOD WAH endpoint security

People are people and it's just human nature to not always be on guard at home, even if this is now our normal workplace. It is important to build data security into the heart of your distributed network and to ensure that when your team connects to the office systems, they can be confident they are doing so securely, even if they are in a relaxed environment.

Let your workers relax and enjoy their job by ensuring that they are always secure, every time they connect. You will always want to maintain a culture of security, but when people inevitably drop their guard, the bumpers will be there to save them. And not only does this keep your customers safe and your data safe – you are also caring for the safety of your employees in the same breath.

## CHAPTER SEVENTEEN:

# HELP YOUR WFH TEAM TO KEEP THEIR ENVIRONMENT SECURE

As mentioned in the last chapter, it is important to design security processes that will function without a great deal of effort. The best protection for customers, and your employees, is when the security is baked into the tools that are being used, rather than requiring extra effort. As we stated, this often means that security protocols are just bypassed.

The security experts Kaspersky, have some good security tips on their website[1] and after reading their advice and blending it with our own experience, we would suggest the following areas need to be reviewed:

- **Physical space:** Encourage and remind your employees to take care on video calls to change or blur your background. Ensure your webcam is covered when not in use. Create a safe physical space where you can work in private without family members monitoring what is on your screen or desk. Use headphones on calls to prevent others overhearing company information. In short, a basic and complete review of the workspace you are using.

- **Wi-Fi:** ensure that your SSID (network name) does not identify you or your address. Limit access to the network by only allowing known devices to connect. Enable network encryption. All the basic steps to ensure that your home Wi-Fi network is as secure as possible.
- **Work Devices:** don't ever allow family members to use work devices. If the kids need another iPad then buy or borrow one - don't let them watch cartoons on a work device.
- **Phishing:** ensure that your team is aware of threats such as phishing - even test them by sending out alerts with an invitation to click on a link. Are they still clicking even when they know the dangers? Coach them in social engineering, the techniques that hackers use to access networks by pretending they are a customer or friend of a friend and accessing information directly from the employee.
- **Storage:** ensure that nothing is stored or processed in the home - all data needs to be in the cloud and only accessed via the secure VPN.
- **Passwords:** it's a basic and boring point, but many people still don't take password security seriously. Use tools that can

enforce greater security and longer passwords if you can.

As we mentioned at the beginning, secure access to a workplace VPN is the single most critical aspect of your WFH security strategy, however many of these other points are good security hygiene and are important. Imagine a contact center agent working from home and talking to customers about their personal finances on a loudspeaker when working in the kitchen with other family members nearby!

Employee training and ongoing guidance is the critical lesson here. You can design secure systems that function with very little intervention, but there is some basic security hygiene that everyone on the team needs to respect. Build this into your onboarding, training, and regular checks.

# CHAPTER EIGHTEEN:

# CONCLUSION AND CLOSING THOUGHTS ON WFH

Do you recall the Choluteca bridge in Honduras we mentioned in chapter five? The sheer irrelevance of a bridge over nothing, with no approach roads, highlights the scale of what the Covid-19 pandemic has created. Will your organization be the bridge or will you carve out a new channel, just like the Choluteca river?

Covid-19 has been the biggest forced global experiment on working practices of all time. Only trained epidemiologists, and students of pandemic history, ever appreciated how this could grow to be so significant so fast. In March 2020 many executives expected a few weeks away from the office, then a complete return to normality after the Easter break.

As we write this final section in April 2021, much of the world remains in lockdown. Many vaccines have been delivered, but countries such as France, the US, and Brazil are all facing the potential for a new wave to hit before enough people are vaccinated to prevent more misery. The end is in sight, but some countries are emerging from the crisis slower than others.

The duration of this crisis has changed consumer behavior and our working practices. New experiences and approaches have been encoded and are become accepted as normal.

When this tsunami recedes, many of these new approaches will become expectations. Our working landscape will no longer feel the same as it was in 2019, just like the Choluteca bridge.

We both hope that you found the information in this book interesting and useful. We really enjoyed putting this book together and there cannot be a more important and relevant subject for all business leaders at present. Working from home was proven to be possible by the pandemic and this will fundamentally change how people work in future.

In this final section, we want to just reiterate some of the key points that have been stated in the earlier chapters. All of the chapters feature useful information, but if you want to take half a dozen key points from this book then we suggest you think about these subjects:

- **WFH is here to stay:** WFH is about much more than WFH. If you read the announcement by Spotify[1] that we quoted at the start of the book then it is clear that the entire culture of the company, remuneration, and management practices are changing. People will be more often rewarded and promoted for what they deliver, creating a far more transparent culture that is entirely different to the office politics many of us have experienced.

Globally, across every industry, any professional office-based job that requires nothing more complex than a laptop will be performed entirely, or partially, from the home.
- **You can no longer hide behind Covid:** in the early days of the pandemic there was a genuine emergency. Corporate executives were surprised to hear politicians announce complete lockdowns that suddenly made it impossible for employees to get to work. Everyone has had more than a year to figure this out. Awful customer service or weak security can no longer just be attributed to the pandemic. There will be no tolerance for this or for the failure of high calibre Business Continuity Plans in the face of any future crisis. You now need to accept that WFH is a core component of what McKinsey is calling 'the next normal.' Build the service and security you need for this new business environment. Covid is no longer an excuse.
- **Your risk profile has changed forever:** we saw risk profiles changing dramatically when cloud-based applications became common, but now you need to accept that your corporate network consists of the cloud, the office, and the distributed workforce. They may partially return to the office, but the most likely scenario is that these employees are going to remain working remotely, using the office as a hub for meetings and socialization. It is essential that you redefine how you view

security - appreciating the view from the outside into the organization and not just the network-centric view from the center to the edge.
- **Decentralize to survive:** All the business services we take for granted, such as email, spreadsheets, and Customer Relationship Management (CRM), are delivered as cloud apps. Now you need to redesign your entire corporate network again to ensure that the distributed home workers are included as an integral and permanent ingredient - they are here to stay. Given what happened in 2020, the importance of the cloud is self-evident, but we also think that a review of all business processes and tools to ensure that are all safe for working from home is an important step - moving on from an emphasis on the network to a redesign of your business processes.
- **BYOD:** we have to move on from the emergency mindset. Employees cannot be hired only when they live in proximity to a contact center or office so laptops and technical support can be locally provided - you need to start thinking how remote working can function for the long-term. Are you really getting into the logistics business and managing the purchase and maintenance of thousands of laptops - with all that means for damage to the environment too? A sensible Bring Your Own Device policy can remove all this complexity from your business, even if you are offering cash grants to employees to

help them purchase equipment. Employers that do not embrace this opportunity may find that they start becoming uncompetitive in the market for talent that become more geographically diverse.
- **Security without thinking:** as we suggested in the introduction, about half of employees will let security standards slip once they feel that the boss is no long watching. Adding cameras and other surveillance techniques may be used by some companies, but it does create an atmosphere of distrust and doesn't necessarily improve security. You need to create systems that are secure just by using them. Once your employee logs into their work system it needs to function like the bumpers in a ten-pin bowling game - your security processes automatically stop you falling into the gutter.

Phrases such as the 'new normal' or 'next normal' felt clichéd in the middle of 2020. Every media outlet was full of analysts all making predictions about which behavioral changes would be normalized by the pandemic. We can now safely say that WFH will be one of the most fundamental societal changes to come out of this.

Not everyone agrees. The CEO of Goldman Sachs, David Solomon, called working from home an 'aberration' in February 2021.[3] This may be his view, but as Shelli Ryan mentioned in her foreword, the adoption of flexible working policies that allow employees to choose where and when they work are becoming normalized. Companies that focus too hard on a return to the old normal risk becoming unattractive as employers.

Mr Solomon's view certainly does appear to be in the minority, even in his own industry. Will companies just be forced to pay more to enforce an inflexible working environment on their employees?

This is a serious point. Employers that now want to attract the best global talent have to offer more flexibility and WFH options. In the US, a Pew Research study published in December 2020 found that 54% of Americans want to continue working from home post-Covid.[4] After the experience we all had in 2020 it would feel odd to brief your HR team that you want to hire a new team member and you expect them to be in the office Monday to Friday from 9am to 5pm.

This just feels extremely dated today. Companies like Thinscale grew rapidly during the pandemic and became used to onboarding and training new team members without ever meeting them. Thinscale - and now many other companies - evolved and embraced practices and systems that are capable of onboarding in this way.

WFH does have downsides. Some employees don't have enough private space to create a workplace at home. This applies most often to younger employees who still live with their parents or share a home with friends. Working perched on your bed isn't very productive.

There are different home structures all over the world. In some regions of the world it is entirely normal for several generations of the same family to live together. In some, it is common for many people to share a large house or apartment. Naturally in all these shared environments background noise can be a problem for home workers. However, there are now tools available, such as krisp.ai aimed at improving call quality and reducing background noise.

The World Economic Forum published research[5] in March 2021 detailing how employees need more help to delineate their time at work and time at home. France already has legislation in place that allows employees the right to "switch-off" from work. This problem of balancing work and home is even more acute when it is impossible to create a separate workspace. Tools like Secure Remote Worker can help to create a delineation as it is not possible to use a device for personal tasks at the same time as business processes.

A study in Germany[6] found that many employees found their work/life balance is worse when working from home, precisely because they cannot switch off. German men are averaging an extra six hours a week working for their employer when based at home and women an extra hour - although women are also managing the majority of childcare as well so they get an even worse deal.

Even before the pandemic, there was a problem with work/life balance. In the US, research from 2019 suggests[7] that 43% of employees check their work emails every few hours - even outside of work hours. Around 10% check constantly, endlessly watching for new notifications.

In February 2020, the European Union Jobs Commissioner , Nicholas Schmit, said that workers need the right to disconnect from their employer - they should not be treated like 'robots.'[8] Mr. Schmit was right then and his point has been further emphasized by the pandemic.

It has always been hard for people to switch off from work, but for many the commute provided a natural break in the day. Just by leaving a place associated with work and spending time traveling home, people can decompress more easily. Home and work are more easily separated.

It is clear that as WFH becomes normalized companies will need to aid their employees with these issues around work/life balance. They will need to 'nudge' the employees. It has been common for several years in Germany for email servers to withhold new email, only forwarding it on to the employee at the start of a new working day.[9] Nudges like this can quickly change behavior - why would you keep checking your work email in the evening if you know the central server will not send anything until the next morning?

WFH and hybrid work will now become the standard for professional employees who were previously office-based so employers and governments need to address these lifestyle questions, but it is worth noting that WFH also has many benefits, such as:

- **No commuting:** not just a great time saver, but also good for the environment and our cities. Many metropolitan areas have seen a huge reduction in traffic. Some commentators, such as Professor Nicholas Stern of the London School of Economics, believe that Covid-19 could be a turning point for climate change globally.[10] Both WFH and the significant reduction in business travel that took place, which is

likely to take years to recover, will be a key driver of this change.
- **Flexible hours:** WFH has introduced more flexibility in working hours, rather than the traditional single 8-hour shift. Start early or take a break to collect the kids from school and then do a couple more hours - it's entirely up to the employee. This flexibility will become best practice amongst the best employers in the world, but will also be table stakes for any company that wants to attract the best talent.
- **Transparency:** because remote supervision is almost impossible the emphasis for managers has been on improving the clarity of their communication, making sure everyone knows what is expected, then letting the team get on with it. People are judged more on what they actually deliver, not who they get on with at the office.
- **Aversion to unnecessary meetings:** people don't want to be on Zoom all day so they are getting choosier about which meetings are essential and also making them shorter.
- **Resilience:** companies across the world have managed to keep going despite the most challenging circumstances. The news over the past year has been filled with heroic stories of beating all the odds and pivoting business models - this pandemic has shown that embracing a distributed workforce can be a key feature of building resilience into your company.

- **Digital connectivity:** potentially one of the biggest benefits of the need to work from home during the pandemic has been how it has shone a spotlight on inequalities in our society and demonstrated that a digital divide really does exist. UNICEF published research[11] in December 2020 that highlighted how the health, friendships, and education of 1.5 billion children across the world are all directly impacted by their access to the Internet and devices that facilitate interaction. When education is online, it is vital that all children, regardless of family income, can access it. The pandemic demonstrated that connectivity and education need drastic reform to be more inclusive.

WFH will change the way that companies secure their information, but the tools are already available. As we have mentioned within this book, ThinScale has worked with companies all over the world and helped them to secure their networks before, during, and after the lockdowns forced employees into their homes.

We both believe that the challenges WFH presents will eventually be addressed though corporate strategy, government and union policies, and a cultural change to accept this as a normal and accepted way of working.

WFH is no longer exceptional. It is normal. Companies that do not offer WFH as an option to their employees will struggle to retain or attract the best talent - it's that simple. In the new normal of the 2020s the key area of focus is how to keep your talent and your customers secure.

# REFERENCES:

**INTRODUCTION**

1. https://www.straitstimes.com/singapore/transport/data-of-580000-sia-customers-leaked-in-security-breach
2. https://www.csoonline.com/article/2130877/the-biggest-data-breaches-of-the-21st-century.html
3. https://www.reinsurancene.ws/data-breaches-threaten-223bn-of-top-brands-value-finds-report/
4. https://www.csoonline.com/article/3410278/the-biggest-data-breach-fines-penalties-and-settlements-so-far.html
5. https://en.wikipedia.org/wiki/General_Data_Protection_Regulation
6. https://www.theguardian.com/technology/2017/oct/27/nhs-could-have-avoided-wannacry-hack-basic-it-security-national-audit-office
7. https://www.independent.co.uk/news/uk/home-news/amazon-fresh-supermarket-ealing-london-b1812423.html
8. https://connect.uclahealth.org/2020/12/10/the-fastest-vaccine-in-history/

9. https://www.ft.com/content/d2ad4ae3-6b40-4051-a6fe-6f8a75924e30
10. https://www.techrepublic.com/article/48-of-employees-are-less-likely-to-follow-safe-data-practices-when-working-from-home/

## CHAPTER ONE: THE BPOS SENT EVERYONE HOME, BUT HOW SECURE IS YOUR DATA NOW?

1. http://j.mp/3uXIyQr
2. https://www.forbes.com/sites/ashleystahl/2020/06/15/what-does-covid-19-mean-for-the-future-of-work/#54523fbb446f
3. https://www.cnbc.com/2016/04/27/most-hacks-take-minutes-to-do--and-weeks-to-discover.html

## CHAPTER TWO: WFH IS HERE TO STAY, SO HOW SECURE ARE YOUR EMPLOYEES?

1. https://www.bbc.com/news/business-52467965
2. https://www.mckinsey.com/business-functions/operations/our-insights/elevating-customer-experience-excellence-in-the-next-normal
3. https://www.forbes.com/sites/jackkelly/2020/05/24/the-work-from-home-revolution-is-quickly-gaining-momentum/#1beae0061848
4. https://www.5ca.com/
5. https://livexchange.com/
6. https://cxfiles.libsyn.com/stephen-loynd-trendzowl-analysis-on-the-new-normal

7. https://www.theguardian.com/technology/2020/jan/21/amazon-boss-jeff-bezoss-phone-hacked-by-saudi-crown-prince

## CHAPTER FOUR: WHICH RISKS ARE ELEVATED AS YOUR TEAM RETURNS TO THE OFFICE?

1. https://www.zdnet.com/article/cybersecurity-half-of-employees-admit-they-are-cutting-corners-when-working-from-home/
2. https://www.zdnet.com/article/going-back-to-the-office-here-are-five-major-tech-problems-that-lie-ahead-of-you/

## CHAPTER FIVE: SECURITY WILL BE THE KEY TO SURVIVING IN THE NEW NORMAL

1. https://www.theguardian.com/business/2020/aug/30/independent-shops-enjoy-business-boost-due-to-commuting-drop
2. https://www.bbc.co.uk/sounds/play/w3csz89s
3. https://www.thedrinksbusiness.com/2020/06/claridges-hotel-selling-fried-chicken-to-go/
4. https://www.thejournal.ie/uk-home-working-5188876-Aug2020/
5. https://securityboulevard.com/2020/06/the-state-of-wfh-security-3-months-in/

## CHAPTER SIX: SECURITY IN AN ERA OF DECENTRALIZATION

1. https://www.fastcompany.com/90614268/its-time-to-start-designing-for-the-future

2. https://www.zdnet.com/article/mckinsey-three-factors-drive-consumer-loyalty-in-the-next-normal/
3. https://www.mckinsey.com/business-functions/marketing-and-sales/our-insights/a-global-view-of-how-consumer-behavior-is-changing-amid-covid-19
4. https://www.mckinsey.com/industries/healthcare-systems-and-services/our-insights/telehealth-a-quarter-trillion-dollar-post-covid-19-reality

## CHAPTER SEVEN: WHAT ARE THE IMMEDIATE SECURITY RISKS OF WFH?

1. https://www.bbc.com/news/technology-52628119
2. https://www.dispatchlive.co.za/lifestyle/2020-09-01-hot-desks-are-here-to-stay-as-the-office-gets-a-makeover/
3. https://www.forbes.com/sites/carrierubinstein/2020/04/10/beware-remote-work-involves-these-3-cyber-security-risks/#1863b0f661c4
4. https://www.theguardian.com/technology/2020/jan/21/amazon-boss-jeff-bezoss-phone-hacked-by-saudi-crown-prince
5. https://www.prnewswire.com/news-releases/thinscale-recognized-as-a-2020-global-enabling-technology-leader-by-frost--sullivan-301118401.html

## CHAPTER EIGHT: THINKIOSK AND WFH SECURITY - A SHOUT OUT FROM FROST & SULLIVAN

1. https://cxfiles.libsyn.com/brendan-kiely-thinscale-waha-the-tech-supporting-working-from-home
2. https://www.linkedin.com/in/michael-desalles-82519114/
3. https://blog.thinscale.com/thinscale-wins-2020-global-enabling-technology-leadership-award
4. https://www.thinscale.com/products/thinkiosk/

## CHAPTER NINE: WFH AND BYOD: DOES IT MAKE SENSE TO SEND LAPTOPS TO AGENTS?

1. https://cxfiles.libsyn.com/michael-desalles-frost-sullivan-covid-19-and-the-bpo-road-to-2021
2. https://www.youtube.com/watch?v=4RogdOyZ-RU

## CHAPTER TEN: WHAT IS THE ROAD TO CX RECOVERY AND NORMALITY IN 2021?

1. https://www.linkedin.com/pulse/what-immediate-security-risks-wfh-mark-hillary-em-/
2. https://www.linkedin.com/pulse/wfh-byod-does-make-sense-send-laptops-agents-mark-hillary-em-/

## CHAPTER ELEVEN: WORK-FROM-HOME IS BECOMING A LONG-TERM CX SOLUTION

1. https://cxfiles.libsyn.com/andrew-mcneile-thinscale-technology-why-wfh-bpo-needs-byod

## CHAPTER TWELVE: THE HYBRID COMPANY HAS ARRIVED AND IT'S FANTASTIC NEWS FOR ALL

1. https://www.weforum.org/agenda/2021/01/hybrid-working-golden-age-of-the-worker/
2. https://edition.cnn.com/2021/03/18/investing/goldman-sachs-analyst-workplace/index.html

## CHAPTER THIRTEEN: YOU DON'T GET WFH SECURITY BY MONITORING WORKERS ON THEIR WEBCAM

1. https://workplaceinsight.net/working-from-home-opens-up-new-data-security-threat/
2. https://www.washingtonpost.com/technology/2020/04/30/work-from-home-surveillance/
3. https://www.cybereason.com/blog/cyber-security-tips-for-allowing-employees-to-work-from-home

## CHAPTER FOURTEEN: WFH IS GOING MAINSTREAM, BUT WILL COMPANIES ALSO EXPLORE BYOD?

1. https://www.linkedin.com/pulse/wfh-byod-does-make-sense-send-laptops-agents-mark-hillary-em-/

2. https://www.personneltoday.com/hr/aviva-to-close-offices-in-flexible-working-hybrid-work-from-home-plan/
3. https://www.nbcnews.com/business/business-news/just-1-10-companies-expect-all-employees-return-office-n1255589
4. https://www.financialexpress.com/industry/offices-2-0-await-employees-this-year-companies-prefer-adopting-hybrid-work-model/2177442/
5. https://en.wikipedia.org/wiki/Deloitte
6. https://en.wikipedia.org/wiki/PricewaterhouseCoopers
7. https://en.wikipedia.org/wiki/Accenture
8. https://ww2.frost.com/news/press-releases/thinscale-recognized-as-a-2020-global-enabling-technology-leader-by-frost-sullivan/

## CHAPTER FIFTEEN: WFH IS THE NEW NORMAL - YOU NEED A NEW SECURITY PLAN NOW

1. https://www.techrepublic.com/article/the-rules-of-work-are-changing-and-we-are-all-struggling-to-adapt/
2. https://hbr.org/2021/02/wfh-is-corroding-our-trust-in-each-other

## CHAPTER SIXTEEN: HELPING RELAXED WFH WORKERS TO BE SECURE

1. https://www.securitymagazine.com/articles/94569-salesforce-becomes-latest-tech-giant-to-embrace-permanent-work-from-home

2. https://en.wikipedia.org/wiki/Salesforce_Tower
3. https://workplaceinsight.net/working-from-home-opens-up-new-data-security-threat/
4. https://www.thinscale.com/products/secure-remote-worker
5. https://www.prnewswire.com/news-releases/thinscale-recognized-as-a-2020-global-enabling-technology-leader-by-frost--sullivan-301118401.html

## CHAPTER SEVENTEEN: HELP YOUR WFH TEAM TO KEEP THEIR ENVIRONMENT SECURE

1. https://www.kaspersky.com/resource-center/threats/remote-working-how-to-stay-safe

## CHAPTER EIGHTEEN: CONCLUSION AND CLOSING THOUGHTS ON WFH

1. https://newsroom.spotify.com/2021-02-12/distributed-first-is-the-future-of-work-at-spotify/
2. https://diginomica.com/companies-shouldnt-hide-behind-covid-19-poor-customer-experience
3. https://www.bbc.com/news/business-56192048
4. https://www.pewresearch.org/social-trends/2020/12/09/how-the-coronavirus-outbreak-has-and-hasnt-changed-the-way-americans-work/
5. https://www.weforum.org/agenda/2021/03/right-to-disconnect-from-work-at-home-eu/

6. https://www.weforum.org/agenda/2019/03/flexible-working-can-make-work-life-worse-germany/
7. https://www.statista.com/statistics/911592/frequency-consumers-checking-work-emails-outside-work-hours/
8. https://www.politico.eu/article/eu-jobs-commissioner-workers-must-have-right-to-disconnect/
9. https://www.dw.com/en/banning-e-mail-after-work/a-17445387
10. https://www.smithschool.ox.ac.uk/publications/wpapers/workingpaper20-02.pdf
11. https://www.unicef-irc.org/publications/1099-digital-connectivity-during-covid-19-access-to-vital-information-for-every-child.html

# APPENDIX 1:

## ALONG THE FRICTIONLESS PLANE: THE CASE OF THINSCALE

Stephen Loynd
Founder and Principal at TrendzOwl
www.trendzowl.com
http://bit.ly/sloynd

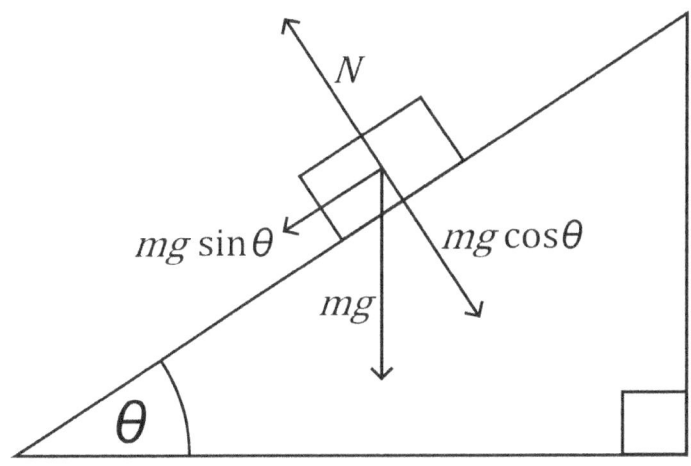

> Innovation, security and end-user experience are at the core of our ethos and act as touchstones throughout the development process resulting in solutions that are lightweight, scalable and solve real-world problems faced by virtualization experts and IT teams every day.
>
> - ThinScale website

Recently I was reading a piece[1] in The New Yorker magazine about the social tumult caused by the bubonic plague of the Middle Ages (the "Black Death"), and how that tragic, cascading event paradoxically helped lead to the Italian Renaissance. At one point the article notes that the Renaissance eventually spawned one of the most influential thinkers in history in the form of Galileo Galilei – the man who established the scientific method. I've long been fascinated by Galileo's concept of the frictionless plane[2] (predictions of an object moving down an inclined plane in a frictionless environment); it was just one of many of Galileo's innovations in physics and engineering.

Today, as we deal with a modern plague called Covid19, the realm of IT just may be experiencing its own kind of Renaissance, an efflorescence of new ways of working, progress for today's increasingly mobile and homeshored workforce along a new kind of frictionless plane. While the concept of "user centric IT" has been around for years, it seems to be gaining renewed momentum under our current circumstances. As author Jacob Morgan put it[3]:

Organizations are now looking at ways to focus on the individual employees by allowing them to use the technologies they want, need and are familiar with based on the technologies they use in their personal lives. User-centric IT will truly allow employees to work anytime, anywhere and on any device.

I was thinking about all this in light of a recent briefing from a fast growing technology company called ThinScale[4]. Founded in 2013 and based in the Media Cube[5] on the IADT campus in Dublin, Ireland, ThinScale offers solution-driven products that aim to help enterprises optimize their virtualized environments and increase productivity while improving security. Its focus is on software-defined thin clients, desktop virtualization, and server-based computing, working to transform the way endpoints are delivered and managed. The objective is to help IT deliver a modern digital workplace and a seamless (i.e., frictionless) user experience.

The company has an international focus across 22 countries with main markets in the Netherlands, the UK, and the United States. It also was featured on a recent April, 2020, CX Files[6] podcast.

## DISRUPTING THE MARKET

Back in 2013, ThinScale sought to disrupt the thin client market with ThinKiosk, the first Windows based PC to thin client converter. A thin client is a lightweight computer that has been optimized for establishing a remote connection with a server-based computing environment (where most applications, data, and memory are stored). In other words, it runs from resources stored on a central server instead of a localized hard drive.

In effect, ThinKiosk turns an existing Windows PC into a secure, centrally managed Windows-based thin client. In so doing, it reduces hardware and management costs while delivering a single pane of glass, allowing IT teams to manage the entire estate of thin client devices and confirm they are up to date, secure, and compliant. It also delivers a unified end-user experience on all converted endpoints. It is compatible with virtual desktop infrastructure (VDI) solutions from Citrix, Amazon, Microsoft, and VMWare, sitting within those provider solutions rather than replacing them (these companies deliver business applications while ThinScale focuses on securing the endpoints of the devices that access such applications).

## A BYOD WORLD: ENTER SECURE REMOTE WORKER (SRW)

In today's environment, business continuity planning (BCP) must include the possibility of future waves of Covid19. Yet even before Covid hit, it was clear to ThinScale that business process outsourcers (BPOs) in particular needed an easy, effective solution for their growing pool of home-based agents operating within a "Bring Your Own Device" (BYOD) model. Unsecured personal devices accessing resources through a similarly unsecure connection to corporate resources (local, virtual, and remote applications and desktops) risked data leakage while offering almost no IT control and no real way to force through updates. Moreover, with distributed hardware-based solutions, companies had to ship products to their remote employees, which didn't work well as an economic model. BPOs were also experiencing high failure rates in supporting external hardware. With a USB delivered operating system (OS), the required stick was often difficult to obtain, and was always prone to not functioning properly.

ThinScale responded to these challenges by developing a unique Validation Tool. Secure Remote Worker (SRW) is a software-defined thin client specifically designed to help enable the BYOD model for Work-at-Home (WAH) programs. The process is straightforward. The lightweight SRW app installs on an agent's personal device. The Validation Tool then assesses that personal device to check if it meets security requirements. Once the device passes the necessary checks, the agent uses a Single Click Installer for the software. In minutes, SRW applies the relevant policies and settings without overriding the device's OS; the device is approved and the agent can log into the SRW session to access remote environments that are centrally managed by IT.

The agents can now access corporate environments, applications, and data while meeting all security and compliance standards. In other words, when the agent is logged-in, SRW provides a secure and compliant workspace. Once the agent logs out of SRW, lockdown policies are lifted and the agent again has full control of their device. Thousands of agents can be up and running quickly, easily, and securely without the need for additional hardware.

As a software-based solution, ThinKiosk and SRW together are designed to run on any Windows compatible device. The former allows BPOs to reuse existing devices, and the latter enables homeshored agents to use personal devices, obviating the need to deliver devices to agents or retrieve devices when they leave an organization. BPOs can utilize the hardware they already own or agents' personal devices. The only cost is the software license.

## SPEEDY SELF-SERVE: ELIMINATION OF WORK FRICTION

What's striking about SRW is the way in which it so easily provides homeshored BPO agents a simple link to access a new way of working. It's a small file with rapid download, taking anywhere from 4-10 minutes to get an agent ready to work. SRW then sits on an agent's PC and does not require a high spec computer. Through SRW, that locked-down personal device is connected to the ThinScale Management Platform for simple self-service device validation. Larger customers can scale hundreds and even thousands of agents per month.

    This is an agent centric model. Device readiness is the responsibility of the agent and not IT support. The software-only system is designed for remote working while also simplifying the targeting of new employees in large cities. Effectively, it expands the hirable population, offering global reach without hardware logistics and a more complicated management platform, easing aspects of administration. Stats are accessible from the central management console. There is no need to buy equipment.

    In essence, Secure Remote Worker offers a high quality, familiar, easy user experience that will do much to improve productivity in the midst of challenging times.

## CONCLUSION: ADAPTING TO AN UNCERTAIN WORLD

In May, 2020, a review of a new biography of Galileo appeared in Nature magazine. "While working in Padua," the piece tells us, "Galileo often visited the nearby port of Venice, where he was introduced to the 'spyglass,' a new-fangled instrument from Holland that could be used to see ships approach. Galileo turned it to the heavens to make the discoveries that changed the course of astronomy."

Not unlike Galileo improving the design of what came to be known as the telescope – such that it could magnify twenty to thirty times – companies like ThinScale are continuing to innovate software-based solutions that offer a scalable, supportable, cost effective, and secure way forward for Work-at-Home programs for global BPOs.

The company regularly adds new functionality to its products based on customer feedback. In that spirit, ThinKiosk and SRW version 6.1 were just released (the same month as the aforementioned book review). There are enhancements to existing control features and additions to the end-user experience. The following main features have been added:

- **Custom Watermarking.** Added to the ThinKiosk and SRW user interface (UI). The watermarking feature acts as a deterrent against data leakage (should photos be taken of screens while in a secure session, they can easily be identified).
- **Resource Searchbar.** Added to the ribbon bar of the main application tab in the

ThinKiosk and SRW UI. Allows users to search through resources available in the application tab. Intended to make life easier on end-users who have a large amount of applications in their secure UI.
- **User Installation & Package Download Indicator.** Enhanced existing software package deployment to allow packages to be installed based on the ThinKiosk User in both SRW and ThinKiosk. Allows software packages to be installed on the machine as per normal, but the software will only be accessible from the ThinKiosk or SRW client. Allows companies to deploy software packages for users without worrying about them accessing these apps outside of their secure workspace.
- **Complete Local Control.** Enhanced the Application Execution Prevention functionality. Companies can restrict application executables from running even on the user's personal session. Allows the restriction of access to any local corporate applications when the user is outside of the SRW UI (before there was no way of stopping this). Enhancement allows more control over personal endpoints.
- **VMware Horizon Support.** The virtual desktop agent provides an added layer of security to virtual desktops and remote desktop session hosts by running checks on the connecting local device. The virtual desktop agent can perform actions such as denying connection if the endpoint

making the connection is not running SRW or ThinKiosk.
- **Profile Conflict Resolution.** In order to make editing profiles for ThinKiosk and SRW deployments easier for IT administration, the new profile validation checks the settings being applied to an SRW or ThinKiosk profile and will provide a warning if these settings run into compatibility issues.

## SRW'S SECURITY & COMPLIANCE

Along with complete IT control, SRW offers a secure connection with no risk of data leakage and the assurance of secure and up-to-date endpoints. The following details are noteworthy:

- PCI, HIPAA, and GDPR compliant
- Independent Cybersecurity Assessment from advisor Coalfire Systems (also the assessor for Microsoft Azure, Amazon AWS, VMWare)
- Detection (inspection of personal device; Windows updates, AV, VM detection)
- Control (secure shell and remove access to underlying OS, admin rights and system keys)
- Prevention (a set of technologies that constantly enforce security policies; write filter, firewall management and application/service whitelisting)

**Image:** A frictionless plane, from Wikipedia (Key: N = normal force[7] that is perpendicular to the plane m = mass[8] of object g = acceleration due to gravity[9] θ (theta[10]) = angle of elevation of the plane, measured from the horizontal)

This article was originally published[11] by TrendzOwl on July 22, 2020. It is reproduced here with the permission of Stephen Loynd:

## REFERENCES:

1. https://www.newyorker.com/magazine/2020/07/20/how-pandemics-wreak-havoc-and-open-minds
2. https://en.wikipedia.org/wiki/Frictionless_plane
3. https://www.forbes.com/sites/jacobmorgan/2015/08/04/user-centric-it-putting-people-before-technology/#1f03059932fd
4. https://www.thinscale.com/
5. http://www.mediacube.ie/
6. https://cxfiles.libsyn.com/brendan-kiely-thinscale-waha-the-tech-supporting-working-from-home
7. https://en.wikipedia.org/wiki/Normal_force
8. https://en.wikipedia.org/wiki/Mass
9. https://en.wikipedia.org/wiki/Gravity
10. https://en.wikipedia.org/wiki/Theta
11. www.trendzowl.com/post/along-the-frictionless-plane-the-case-of-thinscale

# APPENDIX 2:

## SIMPLIFIED CASE STUDIES

We have included a few examples of simplified case studies here just to give a flavor of what is possible when the Thinscale product set is applied to the challenge of building a hybrid, or completely remote, workforce.

For more detailed case studies please visit the latest collection on the 'resources' section of the Thinscale website:

www.thinscale.com/

### CASE STUDY ONE

**CLIENT:** A major global BPO
**THE CHALLENGES**

- Delivering BYOD for work at home agents
- Reducing costs and logistical overheads
- Meeting compliance requirements
- Scalability
- Achieving PCI / HIPAA compliance in a BYOD environment

## THE SOLUTION

- Delivers a dynamic, secure and PCI compliant workspace
- Enhances the flexibility for IT and agents working from home using their own device
- Reduce time, cost and complexity of client management

## THE BENEFITS

- Secure Remote Worker locks down the agent's personal Windows device, ensuring PCI requirements are met at the endpoint
- Agent devices can be assessed for suitability as part of the onboarding process, eliminating the need for time-consuming trouble-shooting
- Removes the need to manage a physical hardware inventory and assets, eliminating logistical costs
- Easily scale up and scale back down work at home agents

## CASE STUDY TWO

**CLIENT:** A major European BPO

**Issues:**

Needed to rapidly accelerate adoption of work-from-home because of the Covid-19 pandemic and BYOD looked like the best way to do this quickly, but security across 29 locations was the question… No WFH knowledge and building everything from scratch on Azure.

**Secure Remote Worker Strategy:**

- SRW was the only solution that met the client requirements
- No extra work was required to meet compliance standards

**Outcome:**
- Intended deployment in hundreds soon scaled to thousands without major additional work work
- Single click deployment facilitated this rapid growth
- Client now says that all future solutions will be tested alongside this WFH solution facilitated by Secure Remote Worker

## CASE STUDY THREE

**Client:** An American Customer Service Technology Provider

The company used a hub and spoke model with devices prepared and locked down at the hub and then delivered to the agent. This was always considered 'business as normal.'

**Issues:**

- **Corporate machines:**
- Costly and time consuming to deliver these machines back to their "spoke" locations for re-imaging.
- IT spent a large amount of time re-imaging these machines
- 30% of agents will require re-imaging when changing customer account
-
- **BYOD hardware:**
- Time consuming onboarding
- Required an entire at-home engineering team
- 25% of machines needed returning to location for repairs

**Use of a Secure Remote Worker (SRW) and Thinkiosk strategy:**
- Logistics costs eliminated – saving $180 - $450K
- Time to hire reduced from 19 days to 4 days (79% reduction in time to hire)

- ThinKiosk allowed changes to devices centrally & re-imaging centrally is seen as a massive benefit from an operational standpoint.
- Only dealing with logistics twice
- Logistics for devices requiring re-imaging eliminated, saving upwards of $540K

**Outcome:**
- Dramatic reduction in operational costs
- Ability to grow and scale faster
- Ability to remotely hire outside the hub network - hire from anywhere

WFH: Securing The Future For Your Organization

by

Andrew McNeile

and Mark Hillary

© Andrew McNeile and Mark Hillary 2021

All Rights Reserved

Published by ThinScale Books

Dublin, Ireland

thinscale.com

www.ingramcontent.com/pod-product-compliance
Lightning Source LLC
Chambersburg PA
CBHW050006230526
45465CB00003BB/1283